WHAT PEOPLE ARE SAYING ABOUT KATHY COLLINS AND THE MYSTIC CHAPLAIN:

"Open yourself and be surprised. A spirit deeper than the words breathes through the lines of THE MYSTIC CHAPLAIN. Author Kathy Collins takes the reader on a most intimate soul quest in which we become part of her life's journey. She is speaking the unspeakable with a unique, yet humble, voice. Her innate dedication to truth and unstoppable courage to explore the mysteries in the most in-depth way possible makes this book a gem for the soul seeker. THE MYSTIC CHAPLAIN emanates essence like the heart itself. Compassionate, inspiring and with a deep love for life. What a wonderful read!"
—Thomas Young, author of *Live Your Momentum*
and International Heart Teacher

"Kathy Collins' memoir, THE MYSTIC CHAPLAIN, is a vivid reminder that we occupy an enchanted world of wonder and benevolence. Her dazzling array of experiences demonstrates our intrinsic connectedness with one another. Kathy's journey shows that love and compassion can open a door to the awareness that our consciousness is infinite, eternal, and one."
—Larry Dossey, MD, author of *One Mind: How Our Individual Mind is Part of a Greater Consciousness and Why It Matters*

"In this stunning memoir, hospital chaplain Kathy Collins offers us deep trust in embracing our life's final chapter with self-compassion, safety and security. And to those who stand in the face of losing a loved one, it gives tender reassurance." —Michael Bernard Beckwith,
author of *Spiritual Liberation* and *Life Visioning*

"Kathy Collins has given humanity a wonderful gift. Reading THE MYSTIC CHAPLAIN: MY STORY will change your perspective about life forever. She shows you how to open your heart to the synchronicity and coincidences in everyday life. These threads of guidance can help awaken your inner voice and unlock your soul's purpose. I am so excited about this book!"
—Jane Doherty,
author of *Awakening the Mystic Gift*

"THE MYSTIC CHAPLAIN is beautifully crafted and elegant. Through her life experiences, Kathy Collins' story reminds us that we are all connected and have a universal purpose. Her words remind us of the power of living in a synchronized world and that we are here to help each other face our life challenges. This is a must-read and wonderfully delivered story of awareness, hope, and love."

—Larry S. Cockerel,
author of *Your* and trainer

D1253683

THE MYSTIC
CHAPLAIN
My Story

THE MYSTIC
CHAPLAIN
MY STORY

KATHY COLLINS, ASC

Henschel
HAUS
publishing, inc.
Milwaukee, Wisconsin

Published by
HenschelHAUS Publishing, Inc.
www.henschelhausbooks.com

ISBN: 978159598-617-7
E-ISBN: 978159598-618-4
Audio ISBN: 978159598-624-5
LCCN: 2018943478

Cover design by Elaine Meszaros, www.emgraphics.net

"Angel of Mercy" and "Angel of Courage"
used with permission from
Joanne Koenig-Macko, www.joannemacko.com

Photos by Kimberly Arneson of K Jay Photos
kjayportraits.com

In Memory Of

my beloved maternal grandparents, Victor and Agnes Lascelle.
Thank you for living your love through the heart and teaching
the gift of nature. Your spirit essence dances in the wind and
the fragrance of the flowers. Until we meet in light.

Contents

FOREWORD

I have always relied on looking up into the sky for both solace and wisdom. The night sky with its stars and changing moon remind me how small I am in this vast universe. Yet, I too, as Kathy reminds us in her book, am a star. I belong to this beautiful, every-changing universe. The day sky, from dawn to dusk reveals to me the diversity of life and its horizons always a reminder that my life is moving in a forward direction. Kathy's story of healing, visions, change and spiritual opening is such a horizon.

Her book and story is an invitation to join her in a "season of her life," where she found a way to move from loss, pain and grief to an opening of her soul to joy and unconditional love. Her story is universal, expansive like the sky, and unique like each sunrise. She shares in her spiritual memoir her journey with cancer to becoming a hospital Chaplain, and how her experiences "broke the chain around my heart and released me from fear and separation."

When I feel separate and alone, all I have to do is spend some time looking up, gazing into the sky. Kathy's story will offer you another sky-like view of life, a reason not to give up; not keep your gaze down. Look up she writes, look up to the heavens and inside your own soul to find your own healing powers and belonging.

Finally, her message shared in many personal stories is one of living life forward. Dark days and difficulties, the trauma of cancer and loss of loved ones can keep us stuck in the pain of our past. She invites us to not only look up but outward toward our future. Keep our inner and outer gaze forward, there's always something good on the horizon.

Julie Tallard Johnson, MSW, LCSW

PROLOGUE

Our world is spinning on its axis as it always has from the beginning of time, yet all our lives are moving in hyperspeed. Ever feel like you don't know how you will be able to hang on? How do we continue on this course?

I look to nature for peace and solace when I feel things are moving too fast. When we step away from the flurry of our everyday lives, we are given something much more valuable than we could ever imagine. The cycles of nature continue just as they always have. Not too fast, not too slow, but just right. Everything nature has to offer us is a gift. It gives us beauty, and it provides us refreshing moments of calm when we take in its splendor. This is the best medicine we can give ourselves to renew ourselves and connect with the Divine—the one who gave it all to us.

Nature speaks to us when we hear the waves of its lakes and oceans as we sit in the warm calming sands on its beaches and when we see the vistas it offers us from its highest mountain tops. The depths of our oceans provide wonders that will lift our souls. It depends on how well we want to use nature and respect it. Yes, nature gives us a hiccup at times, just like life does. Nature and life are reminding us we need to sit up and take notice. We need to see we are all essential in the world.

My love for nature began at an early age while exploring the shoreline of Lake Michigan. It gave me peace and solace when trying to fit in with the changing world around me. This connection stayed with me all my life. My relationship with nature played a huge role when nudged to question my own religious beliefs. Yes, we all struggle with questions of faith, science, and the changing norms of cultures and technology, depending on where we are on the path of our life.

The scholars in all these fields can explain it to us all very antiseptically, but what happens when they can't? This story is a combination of those norms telling us it can happen, but do they really believe it? Like Apostle Thomas, he needed to see it before he would believe his Lord had risen. I too walked in Thomas's name brand of shoes called *doubt*. When I cast off my shoes and put on my sandals to be freer and less confined, the window to my world flew open and transformed me.

I remember the author Thomas Moore, writing about a new vision and how one could create one's own connection to the Divine from materials of the faith of ancient times within our current life. My love of nature along with my insatiable enjoyment of history to explore the reasons for something and why it happened are similar to my spiritual journey of searching for answers. I looked back at ancient ways and alternative methods for healing and wondered why did so many people move away from them for something more formal and structured? Not that any one of these well-formed structures is right or wrong. All beliefs bring something unique to the table of life and soul growth. When we respect everyone's need to maneuver in this world with what works for them, we would all be able to look into the reflective mirrors placed in front of us and see we are all asking the same from everyone else. It's called oneness.

There are many highways built to reach a specific destination on a map. We all don't have to travel the same road to obtain the goal since the end result is the same. The Divine has shown us many thoroughfares in which to achieve our highest potential, to help our fellow man, and to let our souls grow to their brightest potential in honor of same.

We are all dust from the universe the Divine created for us. We all have something to share since we are all teachers for each other. We don't have to have a college degree to earn this role. Our life teachers can show us something new, or they can remind us that our reflective mirror needs an adjustment. I hope the experiences I'm about to share with you in my spiritual journey will resonate with many, so they too will say, "I want to help."

When we realize the power within each and every one of us, our souls become living stars.

INTRODUCTION

Welcome! You have opened the cover to my book, and you are reading my introduction. I'm grateful that you came. I too already know something significant about you. Your heart is open, and your mind is receptive, and I invite you to come in and walk alongside me as I share with you a season of my life. A season filled with disappointment, pain, hurt, loneliness, sorrow and grief that expanded my soul and opened my heart forever to the joy of unconditional love.

My memoir from experiencing cancer to becoming a hospital Chaplain broke the chain around my heart and released me from fear and separation. When I started to experience my mystical excursion, I recited a daily mantra. To start out, it was short and addressed a very exclusive club I sensed was always around me, "Good morning, angels and archangels. Thank you for a beautiful day!" As my awareness and spiritual experiences grew, so did my mantra. From 1994 to 2015, I slowly added on more beings of energy. "Good morning, angels, archangels, masters, ascended masters, spiritual guide Sarah, guardian angel Martha, Holy Mary Mother of God, Holy Trinity—God the Father, Son and Holy Spirit. Thank you for a beautiful day!" It was no longer an exclusive club—we were all "equal," and we were all "one."

My day could be bitter cold, a blinding blizzard, foggy, or raining pitchforks; it just did not matter. It would always be a beautiful day for me, and I was grateful to be a part of it. We all love sunshine, warm breezes, and brilliant blue skies, but to enjoy those perfect days to their fullest, we need to experience the darker aspect of our weather and then be able to see the clouds part and reveal the beauty of the sun. The same goes for our life's journey. We experience the darkness that comes into our lives and then learn to move forward towards the light to understand how strong and important each and every one of us is to each other.

We all need to experience the importance of "oneness" between us and the Divine energy. We can be guided, ever so efficiently to where our souls need to be, if we quietly watch, listen and eventually respond to the lessons on our syllabus of life. The Divine spark that resides within all of our hearts brings about the glorious union of Heaven and Earth.

The next nine chapters are just a few of the things that happened to me along my mystical journey. Some events shown to me did not actually occur until precisely nine years later. The nine chapters I'm sharing with you are some of the unique gifts given to me as I transitioned from the earthly lessons to my spiritual experiences.

Vibrations, dreams, numbers, and visions were ways of communicating with the Universal field of energy and connecting with the beauty of nature surrounding all of us to get me from point A to point B. I experienced remote viewing, instant knowing, and precognition. I heard a mystical sound and felt deep within my heart the need to change my religious beliefs from unhealthy fearful ones to healthy ones filled with the heart's infinite love.

It wasn't easy to share some of the events in my chapters, but as I did, I began to see the common thread between those involved and the soul lessons I needed to learn. I honor all the parts everyone in my soul family played in my life's journey, and what it meant so I could grow and expand my soul. Some have since passed over, and some are still here. Some have not reunited for whatever reason, but I send them love and light every day. Some came into my life for just a brief moment and left an indelible mark on my heart, teaching me what I needed to know to move forward on my journey of light and love.

All souls, while on the earth, need to experience growth expansion by learning new lessons, and also by improving on the old lessons that still need fine-tuning. I was able to step outside of the box of conformity on the earth plane, and I listened to a heart's call to action from the spiritual plane to make this happen.

All the events shared in this book are as real as the air I inhale today. It is my journey through this season of life to experience the negative and grow from it. Call it wisdom learned through trial and error. I learned to turn the fear and pain around into love and forgiveness, and from that, I grew to look at life from within. The side I wanted was to be happy, free of arguments, a give-and-take of life's bumps to get through things together and to have the ability to see the pain of others and help them to find a comfortable corner in the world to smell the flowers of forgiveness. Compassion for others and compassion for one's self are the elixir to the world's healing.

Please come in and put on the pair of comfy sandals I have waiting for you. Walk with me through these nine chapters and continue to let your heart and mind remain open to the synchronistic wonders that are available and bestowed on all of us through our inherited mystic star power energy.

Let me turn the page…

CHAPTER ONE
FULL CIRCLE

"Synchronicity is the coming together of inner and outer events in a way that cannot be explained by cause and effect and that is meaningful to the observer."
—Carl Gustav Jung

Coincidences are for sissies. Coincidences defined by Webster are a remarkable concurrence of events or circumstances without an apparent casual connection. Who hasn't thought about a friend or family member and just at that very moment, the phone rings, and that person is on the other end of the line. Sure it's fun to acknowledge it, "Can you believe it, I was just thinking about you?" and then dismiss it. In the beginning, mine came as a soft summer breeze knocking at my front door asking to be invited in. I slowly opened the door, acknowledged them and didn't dismiss them. The ensuing visits came fast and furious, like a springtime tornado awakening me from my den of winter, and ripped my front door totally off its hinges. When is a coincidence not a coincidence?

❈ ❈ ❈ ❈ ❈

In August 1994, I attended a company business event, of Midwest shoe store representatives, at General Mitchell International Airport in Milwaukee, Wisconsin. The evening dinner was held outside under a large billowing white tent that let the soft evening breeze off Lake Michigan stream through to gently cool everyone down from the hot summer day. As the dinner was winding down to an end, I took out the raffle ticket issued to me when I arrived and checked the numbers. The announcer started to call out the winning prize numbers of various gifts awarded to the lucky ticket holders. Each time a person won, I politely clapped and smiled to acknowledge their good fortune, as I had done at so many other events, and quietly thought, *"How come I never win?"* Out of many incredible prizes given out, six had already found their way to our round dining table for eight. A man sitting across from me said, "Our table has Lady Luck with us tonight." Our entire table of guests erupted with laughter.

The surprise Grand Prize for the evening was about to be announced. To fill the void of time in between, I played my favorite game with the numeral figures printed on my raffle ticket. I added them up and then broke down the total to a single number. I added the first two numbers: $8+1 = 9$; next two $5+4 = 9$; next two $6+3 = 9$; and final number $+9$. Four nines equaled 36, and I then broke down the final total to a single number...$3+6 = 9$. I thought, *"Hmm, lots of nines."*

The announcer quieted the crowd of guests by tapping on his microphone. "Our Grand Prize this evening will be an eight-day trip for two to London, England, including air and hotel expenses." The full tent erupted with clapping and cheering, glassware being abused by silverware clinking against it as others pounded their fists on the wooden tabletops in approval.

The only two left at our table without a prize to take home were another woman sitting next to me and myself. I replied to the guest next to me, "If our scheduled luck continues, you'll be winning the Grand Prize. Before this event, I have never won anything in my life. I couldn't win a bucket of crap if I paid someone."

Slowly and deliberately, the announcer read off the Grand Prize ticket numbers. My eyes followed across my ticket from left to right as each consecutive number was called out.

(1) Got it—*You have the same number as everyone else in the room. What's next?*

(8) Yes—*It's too early to get excited.*

(5) Okay—*You've been here lots of times before—always a bridesmaid, never a bride.*

(4) Midpoint—*Nice to think about winning, but don't count your chickens before they hatch.*

(6) Dreamer—*Maybe Lady Luck really is sitting at our table.*

(3) Going wild inside—*Keep your panties on, girl, you've never gone this far before.*

(9) SHAZAM!—*Where did you go? Can't you see it? Let me confirm it for you, the numbers are 1854639. Tell them it's you for crying out loud. It's your time... TELL THEM!*

I continued staring at my ticket as the numbers were repeated since no one acknowledged the first call of the winning numbers. The lady next to me leaned over to see the numbers on my raffle ticket. "I don't have the numbers, do you?" she asked.

I couldn't speak. My mind raced like a car down the Indianapolis 500 track, my mouth was dry as a cotton ball, and I could not get my vocal cords to vibrate fast enough to scream out the words I had the winning ticket. My entire being was suspended in time as I was feeling utter joyous disbelief. The lady sitting next to me poked my arm and brought me back to reality when she screamed, "You won!"

❄ ❄ ❄ ❄ ❄

September, one month before leaving for London, I stepped out of the bathroom shower equipped with two interchanging sliding doors—one frosted and the other a mirror. The doors were shifted to opposite sides of where they were supposed to be, and while brushing my teeth, the mirrored door was directly in line with the sink to my left. It reflected back to me my left breast nipple was ever so slightly inverted. I thought, *"Great, now my breast is shriveling up. What next will my forties bring?"* Being in a hurry to get ready for work, I blew off the brief visual warning shown to me. Life went on as usual for the next few weeks, and the shower doors were kept in their proper place.

October arrived, and anticipation and preparation for the London trip were anxiously building. My mom, Dolores Collins, was joining me on this adventure, and we were both in countdown mode to departure. A week before leaving, the bathroom shower doors were again shifted to the wrong side and, while brushing my teeth, I glanced to the left and noticed the indentation of my left breast nipple had increased. It went from what I had blown off weeks earlier as being a slight wrinkle to a volcanic crater.

I raised my arm and performed the breast check all women have been told to do regularly while showering, which I was guilty of not doing at all. I didn't expect to find anything because I had just had my yearly mammogram checkup three months earlier, and the result was normal. Much to my surprise during the self-exam, I found a good size lump dead center under the nipple. I had no idea an inverted nipple was one of the significant signs of breast cancer. I've had fatty cysts found on past mammogram tests, but not in this particular area. The cysts were always benign. I immediately went over my crisis mode check-off list of what to do for now:

(1) Don't panic;

(2) Keep your mouth shut, so Mom won't worry;

(3) Don't contact the doctor before leaving otherwise the trip could be canceled depending on the outcome;

(4) Call the doctor immediately when you return from London; and,

(5) If the news is going to be bad, make sure you have one hell of a good time in London.

🦋🦋🦋🦋🦋

Hurricane weather in Boston before our departure caused a 24-hour delay of our arrival in London. Plans we had for taking care of jet lag on our first day in London were scratched. In advance of the trip, I purchased tickets for *Anything Goes*, *Les Misérables*, *Sunset Boulevard* and *Blood Brothers* in the London theater district to fill our evenings with entertainment. Due to our one-day travel delay, we had just enough time to get to the hotel, get settled into our room, freshen up and dress for our first evening performance. We hustled down to the busy street in front of the hotel, and hailed our first London black-taxi-cab, built like a Sherman tank and substantial enough inside to have a Sunday picnic. We arrived at the theater with minutes to spare for the revival performance of *Anything Goes*. We were escorted to our seats located five rows from the stage, so Mom, only four feet eight inches tall, could see everything.

The first half of the play moved along too slowly, and I was much too jet-lagged to enjoy it, but I was thoroughly entertained with Mom's first half bobblehead dance and her occasional loud snorts due to the deep sleep she was enjoying in her reserved seat. Her snorts quickly turned into gentle puffs of air sounding like "*Pua…Pua…Pua,*" as though she was trying to keep an invisible feather airborne with each puff of air released. At intermission, I escorted her out and back to the hotel. We enjoyed, in full and without interruption, the remaining three plays on our list during our stay.

Trafalgar Square, in the early morning hours of a work day, was spirited with residents on their way to work and school. The morning we arrived at the square, Mom stood quietly in the middle of it. I observed her from a distance as she began to turn slowly around with the exactness of a working quarter horse, pivoting on its back legs, as she watched different groups of young children, on their way to their respective schools, pass by on either side of her. The children walked together, dressed in their distinctive colored uniforms. It reminded me of small schools of fish tightly swimming together for safety from the larger looming elements of life around them. Mom had been in the women's branch of the Navy during World War II and loved the crisp look of a uniform. She observed the children pass by with group precision, and smiled with delight as it brought back memories of her WAVE training days at Hunter College in New York doing her precision marching. It was as if she had found a magical piece of gold hidden behind each child's ear, just like the magician produced gold coins from behind her ear the night before at our King Arthur dinner.

Mom took in all the beauty the square had to offer—its sounds, its colors, and its fast-paced movements of the early morning hours. We had arrived at the right place and at the right time because she never stopped talking about it the rest of the trip. This simple daily morning event presented us with mystical hidden treasures of beauty and love that stimulated and enhanced both our hearts.

We stood in queues to see Buckingham Palace and the Tower of London. We rode the Underground Tube to save time getting across London to take in as much as we could see each day. Each morning the hotel served a typical breakfast of beans and tomatoes with a delicious croissant. Not a typical American breakfast, by any standard, and after a few days, we could only eat the croissant. Neither of us could look at another bean or tomato.

No matter what time we returned to our hotel room each evening, we caught up on the world news while enjoying a cup of hot English tea and nibbling on shortbread cookies we purchased in the market during the day. We reminisced about the day's events and strategized about what we would like to see the next day.

Each night, before going to sleep, I checked the lump that had taken up residence in my breast, secretly wishing each time I checked its location, it would magically disappear. As I lay in bed, in the semi-darkened hotel room filled with intermittent flashes of car lights on the walls from the street below, the nightly litany of questions would intermittently drift in and out of my mind. I thought, *"What's waiting for me when I return home—good or bad news? Will I be able to handle it if the report is terrible? What about my son—how will he take it? How will my body tolerate chemotherapy, since it can't handle many over the counter medications as it is now?"*

Mom and Dad were in their seventies and didn't need to be worrying about this at this time of their life. We had already lost one sibling, Michael, and I didn't want to add to their list of pain and loss. I wondered, *"How will I be if I come out on the other side of all of this when it is all over...or will I come out at all...did I wait too long?"*

Curled up on my side in bed with covers half over my face was the only time I let quiet tears fall on my pillow without being found out by Mom in the next bed. As each night passed, my heart told me the crisis mode check-off list was slowly becoming a reality list shifting into survival mode. Deep down I was sure the news wasn't going to be good when I got home. *See you tomorrow night, freeloader.*

Our last day in London was set aside for shopping and finding gifts to take home. We bought a hand-carved clown puppet and discovered our favorite English tea and shortbread cookies packaged in individual tins from Harrods, London's most famous seven-story department store. Before leaving Harrods, Mom needed to use the women's loo and, upon exiting, she became directionally challenged and went missing for thirty minutes. Clothing racks and displays in the store were taller than Mom, and I had to put together an English fox hunt with the management staff to find a sharply dressed woman, 73 years of age, four-foot-eight tall who answered to the name of Dolores Collins.

❦❦❦❦❦

We arrived home in Port Washington, Wisconsin on Sunday afternoon. I had to return to work Monday morning and didn't want to call my doctor from work. I didn't want office cube mates listening in on my personal medical conversation, so I explained my medical discovery to Mom and asked if she would call my doctor and relay my findings and get me in for an appointment sometime during the week. I watched Mom's face turn ashen, and her body became rigid.

She asked, "Why didn't you tell me before the trip? I can't believe you had such a good time and knew this the whole time."

I replied, "I wanted us to have great memories and treasured moments without having them tarnished with the thoughts of fear and what-ifs."

My office phone rang at 8:15 a.m. and Mom had secured an afternoon appointment at 2:00 p.m. My thoughts of fear quickly turned to anger. Questions started coming up in my mind, *"Did someone mess up my earlier mammogram reading? How could the lump be this large so quickly?"* My "Doubting Thomas" attitude was rising to the surface at full speed. I wasn't taking anyone's word for it; I wanted to see the test results for myself. If it's confirmed positive, did I let too much time go by for getting a head start on killing this monster? Placing blame on someone else was much easier than putting it on me and not owning up to my own negligence of not doing regular breast check-ups.

When I arrived at the medical clinic, I was whisked off to the mammogram department for another look-see. I hoped the always painful mammogram test would actually crush the lump, and I could call it a day and go home, but no such luck. When the exam was completed, the radiologist stepped into the room and stated. "You need to see your doctor immediately."

I responded, "She's waiting upstairs for me now. Can I see my last mammogram test and this new one side by side?"

He answered, "I'll send up both results immediately."

The walk back to the doctor's office felt like miles. It was like a dream when you are in a hallway and doors you are trying to get to keep moving further and further away from you with each step you take. I did not want to hear the final result words that would make this pending nightmare a reality. The tone and urgency of the radiologist's voice let me know I was in deep trouble, and now I needed to know just how deep. I sat down in the doctor's office and there it was on the screen—imaged and confirmed as the two mammogram negatives hung side-by-side. The old one didn't show a thing, but the current negative lit up like the star of Bethlehem. The next step was a biopsy of the lump and, when finished, to see the surgeon my doctor had waiting for me down the hall. Medical staff was not letting any grass grow under them. I was on a fast train from one end of the clinic to the other and holding on for the ride of my life.

The surgeon advised me I would need a full mastectomy because of the location of the lump in the mammary gland duct behind the nipple, and the cancer was fast growing. No door number two choice for a lumpectomy. He also brought up the discussion of having breast reconstruction done after everything was over with. I broke out laughing at the thought of it. I was never able to adequately fill a bra except when pregnant with my son. After giving birth, both breasts took a hike and never came back. No one knew if I had a bra on or not, so why would I put myself through this barbaric process. "No, thank you!" For some reason, this no thank you decision gave me a brief feeling of control, while everything else around me was spinning out of control.

My surgery date was set for one week out. A medical port would be inserted in my upper right chest and used to distribute the chemo into my body instead of the veins in my arms. After a month of healing from the major surgery, the chemotherapy regimen would be set in motion. Three different chemotherapy injections were scheduled for every two weeks for six months. One of the major chemotherapies used was glibly called "Big Red" by medical staff because it would cause every hair on the body to fall out, but medical personnel advised me I didn't have to think about that happening for at least two more sessions.

I returned to work two days after the first chemotherapy treatment. By mid-afternoon, my body was so weakened I could barely sit up, much less think. While taking dictation in my boss's office, I stopped writing, reached forward, put my pen and steno pad down on his desktop, and my head followed suit. He rushed out of the office to get help, while thoughts were passing through my mind so fast I couldn't hear the words that created them. They swirled in my brain like an F5 tornado. I was sent home.

Two days later, the hair on my head and everywhere else on my body fell out by the bushel. By the end of the first week, I was officially a bald-headed eagle with no feathers. *Two chemo sessions to lose my hair, my ass!*

By the end of the first week of treatment, my stamina was diminishing fast. Mom and Dad drove me to the emergency room of our nearby medical center. The on-call emergency room doctor was a young man who was smart enough to know he was in over his head when he assessed my medical situation. As my weakend body slid down sideways on the two-seater bench I had come to rest on, he told me he wanted to call in doctors from the medical center who would be better suited to handle my situation. I agreed. As he made his calls, I was quickly placed in an available emergency room down the hall.

As the medical center doctors worked frantically on me, I believed I wasn't going to make it. I heard one of the three physicians in the room say, "I can't find a vein on either of her arms that will work."

Another doctor replied, "Check her legs for something that will work."

While I lay there between life and death, Mom sat silently on a chair in the room with her head down. I asked the medical team to have her sit in the waiting room with my dad. I didn't want her to see another one of her children pass away. Without her uttering a word, I saw Mom look up and shake her head defiantly from left to right with a look on her face I had often seen as a young child and knew instantly should not be questioned, and the doctors sensed it too—she was not leaving me alone.

My situation was threatening, yet my demeanor was peaceful and not the least bit anxious or fearful. My heart, mind, and soul were in complete surrender mode. I was in one realm, and everyone else in the room was in another, yet we were all there simultaneously. A protective barrier, like a clear bubble, surrounded me and emitted a gentle vibration with a low humming tone like the sound of a hummingbird's wings when it is suspended in flight.

I was able to watch and listen to everything that was going on in the room, but the quick movements and verbal sounds of the medical staff no longer meant anything to me. It was as if they were all in an entirely different bubble, just outside my own, and dealing with a different situation that was of no concern to me.

While the medical staff worked feverishly to find a vein somewhere on my body, I happened to look to my left and saw the young emergency room doctor pass by the door of my room. We made eye contact. A few minutes later, the young doctor came to the door, and we again made eye contact and this time he came into the room and came directly up to me. He said nothing to the other doctors in the room, but he asked me, "Is there anything I can do for you?"

I replied, "My head is cold."

He immediately pulled over a goose-necked lamp and adjusted it over my head, so I could feel the warmth. He then left the room.

Eventually stabilized and sent to a nearby hospital, I mentioned to Mom how sorry I was I never got the young emergency room doctor's name to thank him for what he had done. For the next six months, I was bedridden because of the reaction to the chemotherapy treatments, and I had many more trips to the emergency room after each treatment, but I never again saw the young emergency room doctor. I thought about him and talked about him often with Mom. It was as if both our souls were connected by an invisible thread. He was continually in my thoughts during the difficult months of treatment and healing, and I always regretted not having been able to thank him for his gesture of kindness.

❧ ❧ ❧ ❧ ❧

Chemotherapy treatments came to an end, and I was given a clean bill of health for now because one has to reach the five-year milestone to really make it official. At the end of my regimen of treatments, I returned to the medical clinic one more time with a sizeable thank you basket of goodies for the nurses and staff who helped me through this challenging journey. The head nurse welcomed me with open arms upon arrival and asked, "Would you have time to talk to someone who has the same type of fast-growing cancer you had? She is in her thirties, has two young girls, and she's terrified. She's waiting to have her first chemotherapy treatment." I replied, "I would be happy to speak to her."

As I entered the next room, I saw her two girls playing quietly in the children's corner, and she was sitting along the wall with other people waiting to get their chemotherapy treatments. I had mixed emotions as I came through the door to meet this young woman. I knew after my last chemo treatment I would never have to return to this room, yet today I could feel the anxious thoughts of all those waiting to start and the threads of hope others were holding onto, to get through their treatments successfully. I had traveled in their shoes, and I knew what they were experiencing.

I sat down beside the young woman and introduced myself, and my heart ached for her and the journey she was about to embark on. We began to talk, and I could peripherally see someone leaning forward on the other side of her and then sitting back. I didn't make eye contact because I was listening to the young woman's questions. The person leaned forward once more and this time I made eye contact. I've always been terrible at remembering people's names, but I would never forget a face. I immediately said, "I know you." The person replied back, "Yes, I was the doctor in the emergency room when you first came in, and this is my wife."

❈ ❈ ❈ ❈ ❈

"Truly I tell you, whatever you did for one of the least of these brothers and sisters of mine, you did for me."
—Matthew 25:40 NIV

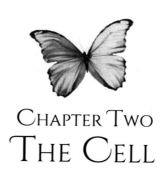

CHAPTER TWO
THE CELL

"There is a voice that doesn't use words. Listen."
—Rumi

Sensitivity to medications is an issue for me. A simple over-the-counter cold tablet would put me into a deep sleep for hours. Chemotherapy was now making an all-out assault on my body and slowly and systematically shutting me down.

Six months of treatment and being confined to bed was a sentence I had accepted. I knew it would be tough, but others in my situation were able to continue with their day-to-day routines and get through it without life entirely coming to a screeching halt. *Why not me?*

When my strength was up to it, I could manage one hour out of my room to take care of hygiene and have my meals. My left arm clung to the left side of my body like a newborn to its mother while breastfeeding. I wasn't able to raise the left arm alone and had to be extra careful of the two tubes jutting out of the left side of my body, with bulbs hanging off the end of the tubes, which looked like the tops of turkey basters, used to collect drainage.

Mom volunteered to help me each morning with hygiene. Our first sponge bath encounter was a learning experience for the both of us. I held out my right arm in front of me for her to wash, and then I lifted it up to the ceiling so she could get at the underarm, and she did it as efficiently as any trained nurse. She proceeded to reach for my left arm, and she lifted it up with the force of a rocket ship leaving its launch pad, and I thought it had a permanent lift-off from my body. I shrieked, "Take it easy, Nurse Ratchet!" When the smoke cleared from the launch, we cracked up laughing at the insane situation we found ourselves in. I affectionately continued to call her Nurse Ratchet, and she wore her new title like a badge of honor.

I would see my dad, William, at meal times because he would not visit me in my room. During meals, I tried to discuss with him my illness and the grave concern I had about how it was going. Dad would immediately put a halt to the conversation by saying, in his stern timbre, "We aren't going to discuss it." It was the same tone I dreaded hearing when growing up. He trained us well to never question him when he used it.

A chasm of isolation grew between Dad and me during my recuperation. The first sign showed up during our first trip to the medical clinic emergency room. Dad took charge when Mom asked him to help get me from the house to the car. He drove with calm composure and did not ask any questions, which was what I needed whenever I was in a crisis mode. Dad helped me exit the car, and I leaned on his firm arm as we all walked into the clinic. When the Emergency Room doors opened up, Dad stopped dead in his tracks and waited in the lobby. Mom continued through the doors with me. I desperately craved his fatherly presence and not getting it silently broke my heart and crushed my soul. I wondered since none of us knew what the end result would be with this cancer, maybe I too was piercing his heart and crushing his soul. *I'm so sorry.*

At home, Mom visited me every day in my bedroom. I awakened from one of many deep periods of sleep, and she was sitting next to my bed reading. I reached out and touched her hand, and my eyes filled with tears as I told her, "This isn't the way it's supposed to be. I should be taking care of you and Dad at this time in our lives, not you taking care of me." I saw her gentle smile and warm eyes as she looked at me, and I heard the unspoken words between us say everything was okay, as I drifted back into another deep sleep.

Options were limited within the confines of my bedroom, which I began to call *The Cell*. Watching television was out of the question. I had no tolerance for daytime soap operas, and no interest in the long, drawn-out media coverage of O. J. Simpson's murder trial that filled the airwaves. Most of my awake time was spent looking at picture books of landscaped gardens of Europe, animals in their habitats, and insects of all kinds, including gorgeous butterflies from all over the world. These books filled the room with artificial sunshine and bright colors during the cloudy days going on outside and also going on inside of me.

I also used music to help pass the long hours of isolation. I had always turned to music to get me through problems in the past and this time was no different. Every day, I played Sergei Rachmaninoff's music. It painted a picture of the dark places I was experiencing with a weighty feeling of the world around me, and as I listened to the urgency of his magnificently complicated keying, it sounded like he too was trying to find his own way out of a dark place. I waited each day for my most desired piece to play, *Rhapsody on a Theme of Paganini, Op 43*. I waited for the precise moment in this magnificent piece to catch the overwhelmingly central music he created. With eyes closed in anticipation, I let it lift me up and out of my Cell on a wave of energy, the size of a tsunami. The music wrapped around me and raised me up to awe-inspiring heights, and then it gently placed me back down on the bed with tender loving gratitude. I imagined myself entering a black hole in space and being jettisoned out on the other side into a bright light of endless possibilities.

❈ ❈ ❈ ❈ ❈

Cancer put on the brakes and slowed me down to an infant's crawl, and allowed me to slowly observe and dissect what was going on around me. My bed was positioned so I could look up and see out the window in a prone position. A 35-year-old elm tree, acting like a Roman Centurion, stood guard outside the window. The late November tree branches were bare of their leaves, and on a good day, they gave me access to seeing blue sky and white clouds pass by like people walking to work in a big city, all too busy to stop or acknowledge me.

Halfway through the chemotherapy treatments, my body was slowly giving up from sheer fatigue because of constant pain in my body. A ride to the doctor's office or emergency room, while comfortable for Mom and Dad, was pure torture for me. I experienced everything the tires absorbed from the road and what they absorbed came through the car into my body like bolts of lightning. I cried out in pain for Dad to slow the vehicle down, thinking it would help, but it didn't. Exhaustion was overtaking my body and shredding the thin thread of hope I had left along with it.

I telephoned my sister, who had retired from the nursing field of Oncology and shared with her my concern I no longer felt I had the stamina to fight the big fight. I finally made public my deepest fear that I wasn't going to survive this ordeal and needed to know if I was right or not. With firmness, she responded, "You are in the depths of Hell right now, but you have to believe you will be able to climb out one step of the ladder at a time." That night, I lay in silence and pondered the words she said to me, and thought, *"Where does one find the physical and mental intensity to endure the fight back up the ladder when one doesn't have anything more to give?"*

In my hours of silence, I befriended a cellmate *Awareness*, found deep within my being. I believed this disease put up a roadblock I didn't trust I could maneuver around or away from, and out of nowhere, *Awareness* whispered, *"Why?"*

Not able to openly talk about my disease with Dad made me feel I was of no value. I had to meet his wishes by being silent in his presence, but what about mine? Another piece of my soul was being chipped away from my not being able to voice my concerns. Dad had an alcoholic father who came from an Irish-American background and Dad had learned early in life how to keep the family secret of alcoholism quiet. He had learned to let his unspoken frustrations grow into anger and resentment, and his life's pain story overflowed into our family's upbringing.

During my youth and early adulthood, I held in a lot of anger and resentment for not being able to express myself, and because of it, felt invisible, not valued, and not respected. The old agreement of "secret silence" from Dad's upbringing was again being imposed upon me now in my greatest time of need.

Dad was not an alcoholic, but his anger, resentment, and frustration from his life's pain story was something to fear in our family. While growing up, a common occurrence at our family meals would be Dad arguing with my older brother about how he could have done something in the sport he was participating in better than he already had. In high school, my brother participated in baseball, football, basketball, and track, so these constant meal disruptions continued year round.

The anticipation of disruption to our family meals made me feel physically ill before getting to the table. As a family, we walked on eggshells waiting for Dad to unleash his fury. I no longer could handle the arguing and berating of my brother, and I stood up from the dinner table and begged, with a levee of tears streaming down my face, "Dad, please stop this!"

As soon as I said it, I knew all hell was going to break loose in my world. Dad, sitting directly across the table from me, stood up in a volcanic eruption. He kicked his chair into the wall behind him and pounded his fist on the table with such force it made the dishes and silverware jump simultaneously, and in a loud condescending voice, he said, "Who the hell do you think you are?"

I replied swiftly with a firm declaration for the family to know and hear for the first time from my lips to their ears, "I'm no one." I knew I no longer wanted to live in anger, resentment and "secret silence." I wanted to be heard and valued, but it would take another twenty-five plus years to finally be able to explore the concept and learn to live it now in my Cell.

The loneliness in my Cell was heartbreaking. I had not experienced this deep emotion since I lost the companionship of my brother Michael. Michael was nine months old, and I was three. I never understood our deep connection for the brief time we had together on the earth, but it was so deep-seated for me, and I remembered with great detail all our times together.

Our last morning together, Michael was lying in his bassinet, and I stood guard in front of it, as Mom stepped aside to grab Michael's morning bath towel. I loved being able to shield him. I would reach up and feel his warm, soft arm and tickle it so I could hear him giggle with absolute delight.

That morning, Michael left the house with Mom and Dad, and I anxiously waited for his return. Mom and Dad returned, but Michael wasn't with them. The agreement of "secret silence" was imposed upon us for the first time I could remember. It was a quietness I never experienced before, and it was genuinely unsettling.

I saw Michael three days later, only this time he was in a room with many people, and he was in a small white bed with beautiful flowers around him. I was tall enough to stand on a riser in front of his new bed. I was able to reach up and touch his arm, only it was cold and hard, and Michael's eyes were closed, and he did not giggle. My hand was slapped for touching him, and I was lifted up and away from my brother by a relative.

This loss and separation created a well-hidden fissure within my being. Michael had been born with a cleft pallet. When he went in for surgical repair, we lost him. I didn't understand at three years old what a cleft pallet was, and through my eyes as a child, I never saw anything different about him. *To me he was perfect.*

❈ ❈ ❈ ❈ ❈

In my Cell, *Awareness* was pulling on me like a rubber band and stretching me to my limits. It was making me feel the pain of cancer, but also my own life's pain story. I was leaning into the pain of both and facing the darkness placed in front of me. I was finding my footing and progressing forward through my fears toward a light on the horizon with a renewed feeling of hope. While stretching me, *Awareness* strengthened me for the surrender and acceptance of what was ahead and prepared me for when the time would come to release me.

The past was over with, and I had to let go of any anger, resentment, and loss I had inside of me and move on. I needed to deal with the *Now* by concentrating on putting all energy, what was left of it, into me and my needs. This was a whole new concept. I never felt I deserved wanting something for myself. I was always aware of the needs of others and would let my needs slide to the curb, thinking they would cause a burden on someone. Asking for something had always been a difficult task. I needed to find my own self-trust and have faith I was worthy, so I began to engage in intimate conversations with the Divine, asking for help. I put a sincere plea out for consideration, in line with many others in the world assuredly more deserving and in need than me, but I had to believe I too counted.

Awareness taught me the importance of compassion and to know my illness, while painful to endure, would help others learn the meaning of compassion for someone else. I always felt great inside after helping others, but not allowing myself to accept help cut others off from feeling great inside, too. Compassion is the most significant gift we can give to each other, to the world, and to ourselves through self-compassion. True compassion comes directly from the heart with unconditional love.

The importance of thinking and being in the *Now* was exposed to me daily. The cold Wisconsin winter days and nights allowed me to hear the house moaning as its wood expanded and contracted from the arctic blasts. After a snowstorm, I listened to the symphony of the neighbors' snow shovels scraping against the sidewalk and the loud tractor sounds of those fortunate to have snow blowers. I was ecstatic the first time I caught a glimpse of a stately red cardinal resting ceremoniously on the Roman Centurion's tallest branch. I was intensely made aware of the little things that happened to me and around me and was grateful to have them be a part of my existence in the Cell.

With the help of *Awareness*, I found the hidden energy to conquer each step of my ladder out of the depths of Hell. The absorbing education received in my Cell came from what I called the University of the Divine, with *Awareness* as my master teacher. The most important lesson was my need to accept and embrace change. I was retrained to remember how to appreciate all that could be heard, felt or seen and most important of all, that which could not be heard, the beauty of silence, and a greater appreciation for what it can create. In my silence, without any secrets or judgments, I listened to my heart beat through restful alertness. I began to witness a change I was willing to embrace, and I wanted more of it. Each day given to me was a blessing, and it strengthened my thread of hope as I surrendered to my needs and the needs of my soul.

Each day in the Cell, I watched the simple ebb and flow of the Roman Centurion's branches moving in the wind outside my window. Its trunk was sturdy and could withstand the harsh winds of winter and early spring. Branches danced around to keep it balanced as its roots held firm deep within the heart of Mother Earth. Some weakened branches fell away, which were needed so the whole of the tree could continue to be strong and experience new growth. The tree spoke to me and showed me how I too could rid myself of unwanted branches to grow healthy.

Awareness confirmed that my disease hadn't put up the roadblock. It was my own fear, anger, and resentment of living in secret silence and not valuing myself, and understanding I wasn't alone. Acknowledging the barriers and understanding what *Awareness* had to teach, I released my pain story, thus making room for my soul story to emerge with the powerful energy of a new star forming in the Universe.

The presence of *Awareness* opened the door to new prospects. I was grateful for every breath I took, looking at each day as a blessing and renewal, and realizing how my illness helped others learn the meaning of compassion. I realized how interconnected I was with nature and those around me and understood health and happiness could emerge when my heart opened up to accepting love and living in gratitude.

Religious conformity and religious family agreements handed down from generations long before me, from our Irish-Celtic and Native Indian backgrounds, started to tilt off-center. My Catholic upbringing would remain a part of my religious experience, but an internal nudge was guiding me to step out of the box of conformity of ritual and doctrine. Something was stoking the fire of my intellect and beginning to systematically rock the core of my inner being.

Awareness was taking me outside the confines of the church edifice where I had been taught, and showed me another connection to the Divine from ways that had been lost with time. *Awareness* showed me that my spiritual center could not be handed to me by others; I had to find the center and make it grow in strength from love and compassion, not fear.

Awareness made me realize the significance of how everything in the world was connected and how the world's cry for compassion needed to be understood and to not look for gratification by how much money or success one can obtain. *Awareness* is like the wind—you can't see it, but you can feel it, and it was intensifying.

Two significant battles were simultaneously going on inside me—one for the return of physical strength and well-being and the other for growth and purpose of my soul.

ﾐ ﾐ ﾐ ﾐ ﾐ

"And be not conformed to this world: but be you transformed by the renewing of your mind that you may prove what is the good, and acceptable, and perfect, will of God."
—Romans 12:2 AKJV

CHAPTER THREE

WINDS OF CHANGE

"In every walk with nature, one receives far more than he seeks."
—John Muir, Naturalist, Author

Going back to work after six months became a reality in May 1995. I was ready to return to the hustle and bustle of the workday world and interact with people. After being warmly greeted by co-workers, I was asked to meet with the Human Resources Director. Upon entering her office, and her welcoming me back, she got up and closed the door behind me. My gut told me something didn't feel right about this meeting. The director advised me that I would no longer be supporting the president of the company. I couldn't believe my ears. I thought, *"Where did the rug go that was just under my feet?"*

This change was unfair in my swirling and questioning mind, especially without prior notification. I kept my questioning remarks to myself and listened to what the director had to tell me. She stated, "Due to the president's job demands during your long recovery, he needed to have a permanent assistant in place." I wondered if he had an issue working with someone who didn't have eyelashes, eyebrows or a full head of hair representing him.

Picking my pride up off the floor, I listened to what else she had to say, "Would you consider supporting the vice-president moving forward?" This was not at all what I expected on my first day back to work, but it was something I had been musing about for the last six months. It was time to let go of the norm and accept change. Like the elm tree, I was being asked to prune one of my branches so I could continue to grow. It was now time to put up or shut up. *"What's it going to be, Kathy?"*

The shift from striving for more of something to just dealing with the moment and being content with it had begun. I didn't know where my new growth was going to take me, but I was willing to trust and let my new path reveal itself in time.

✖✖✖✖✖

When I arrived home, I wanted to tell Mom and Dad about my pruned branch, but Mom had other plans. Mom asked, "Can you sit down? I need to talk to you about something." We sat down at the kitchen table, and I knew from Mom's facial expression that something serious was on her mind.

"I want to talk to you before your dad gets home. Your sister has asked us to move to Sun Prairie now that you are over your cancer and back to work." Mom looked directly at me with her lips pressed tightly together, and her eyebrows rose up on her forehead waiting for my response to this bombshell announcement.

I replied, "I don't have any issues with you and Dad moving if this is what you both want to do." Mom's forehead and eyebrows crunched down like there was more she wanted to say and didn't know how.

"What's up, Mom?"

Mom replied, "She wants you to come with us." Talk about a deer caught in the headlights. I called Port Washington home.

She requested, "Just think about it and let me know. Your dad doesn't know it yet, but I will not move without you." *No pressure here.*

I'm sure my sister had Mom and Dad's best interest in mind when she asked them to think about moving closer, as Mom and Dad were getting up in age. They were still very active and healthy, but life could change in a moment, as we had all learned from my recent encounter with cancer. Being able to be closer to two of their young grandchildren had to have been a tempting carrot dangled in front of them as well.

Was this another branch being marked for trimming on my tree of life? I didn't have anything holding me to Port Washington, but I would need to secure a job in the new location before I would commit to a move. I wasn't sure finding a job would be easy with only a quarter inch of peach fuzz on my head. Wig shopping would be first on my agenda of things to do.

I didn't have the commitment or dedication to my newly assigned boss that I would otherwise have brought into my deliberation about leaving. My previous boss/employee relationship had been broken, and it gave me the freedom to move forward with no loose ends to tie up.

A week later, an interview had been set up for a Human Resource payroll position at a medical clinic in Madison, Wisconsin. I pulled on my newly acquired auburn wig and hit the road for a two-hour drive to our State Capitol.

My potential future boss, Sandy Vanko, Human Resources Compensation Manager, questioned, "Do you think this job will satisfy your needs, based on your past work record skills? You'll be taking a considerable pay cut."

I replied, "I'm looking for a slower-paced environment so I can be guaranteed an eight-to-five work schedule. I want to be able to devote my extra energies and time, outside of work, to help my parents acclimate to their new surroundings and to be there for their needs. The pay rate is comfortable enough for what I need."

My new wig passed the interview test, and Sandy hired me on the spot to start my new job in June, with the understanding that I had to pass the company health exam. The medical review followed immediately after my interview, and I held my breath, hoping they would not ask me about cancer, but they did. I continued to hold my breath, that it would not interfere with my job offer and it did not.

I was anxious to share my good news with Mom and Dad and confirm I would move to Sun Prairie. Upon arrival at their home, I found Bob, the realtor Mom and Dad had hired to sell their home the day before, sitting in the kitchen. When Bob saw me walk in he said, with a huge smile on his face, "Kathy, the house has been sold."

I thought he was yanking my chain, "Right, and I have a bridge to sell you, Bob."

He assured me, "No, it's true." The house had been on the market for 24 hours. I could not believe how quickly everything was moving us forward.

Through the remainder of May, we packed what we could not live without, threw out the things that no longer had usefulness, and donated many items to charity. All three of us were pruning our individual trees before the up-coming move in June. There wasn't any hesitation from any of us to accept the trimming of all our unneeded branches. The winds of change were beginning to pick up speed.

❉ ❉ ❉ ❉

On Saturday, June 24th, the moving van pulled up to our new address in Sun Prairie. Everything went along smoothly for the morning portion of the move-in. Mom and I enjoyed that we did not have to lift and carry any of the boxes or furniture. We stood around and pointed to which room and where things should be placed. It was a cushy sidewalk superintendent job, and we were up to the task. Dad enjoyed talking and joking with the movers and having some male companionship for the day.

At noon, Mom and I stepped outside to take in the beau-tiful warm weather we were blessed with for our move-in day. The noonday sun was radiating its warmth, so we both stood under a shade tree between our house and our new neighbors. We watched the three movers position them-selves on the edge of the moving truck that opened on its right side to eat their hand-packed lunches and get some well-deserved rest and recuperation for the next hour.

While Mom and I stood under the shade tree, we were interrupted by deafening screeches. Neither of us had ever heard a sound like that before. We immediately turned in the direction of our backyard and looked up into the air. Two red-tailed hawks were fighting in mid-air. To see them fighting was an unexpected oddity. The hawks circled and clawed at each other while their wings thrashed for control and position. It was a helpless feeling to stand and observe the laws of nature unfolding before us.

While watching them, I saw an intense flash of light up and to the left of the birds. The bright flash reminded me of someone taking a photo with an old flashbulb camera. I looked in the direction of the illumination and saw a large silver disk suspended in the air. It was not an area of the sky one would typically be looking up at during the day, due to the strength of the sun's light and the damage it can do to the human eye.

I reached for Mom's arm and pulled her over to me. I had her stand directly in front of me with her back to me. I extended my right arm out and over her right shoulder and pointed up at the hawks and asked her, "Mom, follow my finger from where the birds are and up towards the direction of the sun, but don't look at the sun. Just look to the right of it." She started to shake her head up and down in a confirming manner. She turned towards me with eyes the size of half-dollars.

I asked her, "Do you see what I'm seeing?" She nodded her head yes and remained tongue-tied. At that moment, the fighting hawks were silent and nowhere to be seen.

I read a book in the 1970s called *Chariots of the Gods* by Erich Von Däniken. It involved the hypothesis that the technologies and religions of many ancient civilizations were given to the earth by ancient astronauts who were welcomed as gods. I remember the book stirred up thoughts of whether or not we really were alone in the Universe but never did I think I would actually get to see a silver disk in my lifetime. *What was it doing here? Was it using the energy of the sun to refuel? Was it hiding to observe our military air base in nearby Madison? Was I supposed to see it?*

I have always been aware of hawks in my travels along the highways as they stood their ground on the highest telephone poles defending their territory and swoop over the top of my car at windshield level. Seeing a hawk instinctively reminded me of my brother Michael and I would acknowledge him with a smile and a hello and sometimes, depending on how my day was going, I would tell him how much I missed him.

Seeing the silver disk did not unnerve me, but I wanted to confirm its existence further by asking someone else other than Mom if they could see it, too. I strolled down the driveway toward the movers having their lunch. "Hey, guys, humor me for a moment. Can you all look up to the right of the sun and let me know what you see?" Every one of them jumped off the edge of the moving van simultaneously when they saw the silver disk. They all commented on its location as a great place to hide from sight. None of us felt the need to contact the authorities about the sighting. We all agreed we were not alone in the Universe and had seen something phenomenal to confirm it.

The silver disk remained in its suspended position for most of the hour. Periodically, Mom and I would look up and check its status. Before going back to our task of continuing to move in, we looked one more time, and it was gone. It was never mentioned the rest of the day. I didn't tell Dad, and neither did Mom, and I didn't hear the three movers talk about it either.

My Native Indian background on the maternal side of my family and Irish-Celtic on the paternal believed the hawk to be a messenger of wisdom. The hawk played a significant role in their ancient Shamanistic practices, as it was capable of traveling between worlds. The same is true of other ancient cultures around the world.

To have a hawk totem means your vision goes beyond the physical and gives you the ability to see into the souls of people you dealt with. It shows you what is going on in the hearts of people and you are made aware of omens and spirit messages. An integral part of Shamanism is shapeshifting, by which animals can tell a Shaman what he or she cannot see.

Witnessing the hawks and the brilliant flash of light created a stirring of consciousness within me of the connectedness of the ancient past and the present. The fighting red-tailed hawks reawakened and reminded me of the two major battles that were going on inside of me during my time in the Cell and needed to be addressed.

Having Mom and the movers confirm they saw the silver disk helped to alleviate any "Doubting Thomas" pangs I may have had, had I been alone. *Welcome to Sun Prairie!*

ӂ ӂ ӂ ӂ ӂ

I wasn't as healthy as I had hoped after our move and for the next few years. Each day that passed, I experienced continued throbbing pain throughout my body. Some days were better than others, but never a day or night without it. The pain slowly and systematically continued to increase. Family practitioners, internists, and bone specialists were sought out, and every test I was given came back negative as to why.

Every morning before getting out of bed and every night when I got back into bed, I said, "I want to go home." The first time I said it, the use of the word "home" puzzled me. I knew I did not want to return to Port Washington so why was I using the word "home"? Was my subconsciousness trying to tell me something?

It had become difficult for me to do stairs and the simple movement of getting up from a chair was painful. If I sat for any length of time, my body would lock up like a steel vault. Trying to get my body to unlock and move again was equivalent to being hit by the mighty hammer-wielding Thor, the god associated with thunder, lightning, storms, oak trees, and protector of earth.

At night, when it was time to go to bed, Mom and I would turn all the lights off downstairs and head for the stairway leading to our second-level bedrooms. I dreaded the nightly climb. Mom would be at the top of the stairs, and I would only be stepping onto the second stair. It was a real-life story of the tortoise and the hare. I would look up at her as she stood and patiently waited for me to catch up with her each night, and say, "It's not fair you can move faster than me."

❃ ❃ ❃ ❃ ❃

A few years later, I was scheduled to have a surgical pro-cedure, so I had the required pre-op tests, and received a phone call shortly after advising me the surgery had to be postponed for a month. The tests showed my thyroid wasn't working correctly, and I was told I would not survive the anesthetic for the surgery. Chemotherapy had messed up my thyroid and caused every muscle in my body to scream in pain. Why no one ever thought to test my thyroid before this was beyond me.

My health returned to normal as the thyroid medication took hold and did its job, but one area of my life was still wavering—the traditional practice of my religion. Our neighbors, Mike and Gert Lukens, inquired why I wasn't in church with Mom and Dad on Sundays, and I answered the best I knew how, "I'm a twofer." Seeing their perplexed faces, I explained, "I only go to church on Easter and Christmas." I was still hanging onto some of my family's religious teachings and agreements, but was not entirely ready to let go and acknowledge my own center and truth.

I believed as firmly now as I did in my Cell, I did not need to be in a physical structure to connect with the Divine. Slowing down my life helped me take notice and give thanks daily for what was around me. I appreciated the Divine in everything. I found it in colors, beautiful flowers, bird songs, warm, gentle breezes, the smell of the earth after a soft rain, and a prism drop of dew on a flower in the early morning light. I saw it in the energy of light emitted from the bright stars beautifully positioned in the dark velvet night sky, and in a smile on a stranger's face when saying hello in passing—all riches for the taking from the Divine in the world given to all of us. Dad often told me as a young girl, "The best things in life are free." I now understood it and believed it.

Easter Sunday was approaching, and Dad asked me to attend mass with him. Upon entering the church, he started up the aisle and walked past his usual spot next to a pillar in the back of the church that had enough space for two people to sit. Instead, he headed further up the aisle and I followed along. This was an unexpected game change, and I hadn't gotten a pre-game change-up notice. Along the way, we passed our neighbors Mike and Gert, and Dad acknowledged them with a nod of his head. As we continued further up the aisle, I questioned where he was going to stake his final claim for a seat. He proceeded to the front pew. I thought, *"Are you kidding me?"* As I sat next to him, I looked around and glanced up toward the ceiling and mused, *"The walls and ceilings look secure; they won't be falling in on me today."* I waited for the service to start and wondered if I would be moved by a rousing sermon and maybe my thoughts would somewhat soften about the ritual of mass and the need to be within the confines of the building to learn the lessons taught. The celebration of mass ended, and my thoughts remained unchanged.

While Dad drove me home from church, I thought about his unusual decision to take us up to the front pew. While neither of us was on the same page about where to sit in church, our souls were in sync, and they knew he needed to take me as close as possible to the most sacred part of the church. My heart knew I needed to let my mind's eye see, without any distractions in front of me, what direction I needed to take to resolve the battle within me and trust where the winds of change would take me.

For me to leave the church and all its agreements handed down from family members who had come long before me, I needed to present myself in full view and with a clear conscience so I could leave this sacred place with honor, respect, and gratitude for all that it gave to me. The fatherly strength and presence I had longed for most of my life from Dad on the Earth Plane were given to me in abundance on this very extraordinary Easter morning on the Soul Plane as he directed me to that front pew and stood beside me.

I decided the ride home from church would be the perfect platform for me to tell Dad how I had been struggling with my faith and its agreements. "Dad, while I was fighting cancer, nature showed me a beautiful, meaningful, and intimate way to connect with the Divine, and I no longer can do the Sunday church ritual. The church service is not speaking to me the way I need it to. Something's been missing for a long time, and I hope you'll understand. I'm more fulfilled being out in nature and appreciating all that it has to offer. It continues to fulfill me and brings me closer to the Divine in everything I see and touch and not just for one hour on a Sunday morning, but 24/7."

I expected him to close down my conversation in his usual manner of not wanting to talk about it, but he remained silent. His silence led me to assure him, "I will always believe in the Divine and respect what the Catholic Church has meant in my life." When his silence continued, I reminded him of the story he told Mom and me on the 50th anniversary of World War II in 1995.

It was the first time Dad opened up and started talking about the war in detail. He told us his Naval ship had been called to the area of the *U.S.S. Franklin* aircraft carrier after it had been crippled by the Japanese in the Pacific in 1945. He told us he was standing on the top deck of his ship, next to a chaplain, as he and others on other ships assisting the *U.S.S. Franklin*, witnessed over 700 fallen seamen and airmen drop off the side of the *U.S.S. Franklin* to their final resting place. Dad asked the chaplain, "What happens to the Catholics who died without a priest?"

The chaplain replied, "It doesn't matter, we are all one."

The words of the chaplain buried in time had resurfaced 50 years later. They were now a battle cry rising up from within my soul. *We are all one!*

❈ ❈ ❈ ❈ ❈

A friend of mine, MaryAnn Dennis, had knee replacement surgery, and I wanted to get something to help her pass the time while she recuperated in the hospital and at home. We had known each other for a couple of years, and recently MaryAnn had shared with me she had psychic abilities. She told me one of two things would happen when someone she knew passed away before it was officially announced. Her house would fill up with an overpowering scent of carnations, or she would hear her front doorbell ring during the early morning hours, and no one would be at the door. I had never met anyone who had these abilities, and it fascinated me.

I stopped at the bookstore to see if there would be something I could find that might interest her regarding her capabilities. I was directed to the Spiritual/Metaphysical section. I didn't know where to begin, so I slowly ran my fingers across the spine of the books, and read the titles as I slowly moved along the bookshelf. I stopped when my hand touched the book titled *Life on the Other Side* by Sylvia Brown. I experienced a vibration that went from my fingertips, up my arm and then up and down through my entire body like a generator sending a current through electrical wires. The vibration was accompanied with the same humming sound of a hummingbird's wings, like I had heard the first time in the emergency room. Only this time it wasn't coming from around me, it was running through me. I pulled the book off the shelf and bought it.

I read the book before I wrapped it for MaryAnn. The author referenced "Heaven" and "The Other Side" as "home." When I read the references to "home," my mind went into reverse hyperspeed to when I recited my daily mantra, "I want to go home." The use of the word "home" resonated deep within me and warm tears slid down my cheeks the moment I read it. I closed the book on my lap and sat quietly wondering what or who was calling me from a distance, like a voice through a thick fog on an inland lake, wanting me to remember a place I'd been to before and left it behind—and now longed to find a way to return.

I delivered the book to MaryAnn in the hospital, and when she pulled it from the gift bag, she replied with delight, "How did you know I wanted this book?"

꙰ ꙰ ꙰ ꙰ ꙰

I revisited the bookstore a short time later to see if I could get another book written by Sylvia Brown that would interest me. I ran my fingers across the spine of her books and read the titles as I slowly moved along the bookshelf. Touching the book *Past Lives, Future Healing*, I felt the same vibration and heard the familiar humming sound. I purchased the book.

A week later, on a Sunday afternoon, my body started to hurt all over with intense pain. I rested on the living room couch and tried to move as little as possible during the day. The pain was a reminder of what I had experienced after cancer. I wondered if something serious was happening to my health. I went to bed for the night and decided I wasn't going to work the next day. Something was definitely wrong. I woke up Monday morning with severe lower back pain added to the overall body pain I was already dealing with. The lower back pain was not a stranger to me. I often dealt with it through the years, but this time was the severest I had ever experienced.

I stayed in bed and slept until mid-afternoon, and the overall body pain had disappeared, but the lower back pain was not letting up. I propped up my pillows and decided to continue resting in my room and started to read my newly purchased Sylvia Brown book. One chapter was about cell memory, and how much of one's present life is informed by one's past life experiences, and how many unexplained illnesses could be traced back to previous life experiences and how to resolve them.

The chapter had a cell memory prayer inserted within it. I read over it and continued on a few pages further into the book, and something made me go back to the page with the cell memory prayer, and I read it this time out loud. Instantly, I experienced radiating heat throughout my lower back, and it felt awesome. I knew something was different, but I wasn't sure if it would be helpful or troublesome for my back.

That evening I joined Mom and Dad at the dinner table and told them what had happened to my lower back. "It feels like someone opened me up and stuffed a heating pad inside on extra-high heat." Mom came around to my side of the table and touched my lower back and confirmed the heat was searing through my robe and pajamas. Not knowing what I was dealing with, I returned to bed and would decide in the morning if I needed to call for a doctor's appointment. The heat continued to radiate until I fell asleep. I woke up Tuesday morning, and both the lower back pain and the intense feeling of heat were gone.

ꚍ ꚍ ꚍ ꚍ ꚍ

Diane Reinen, another special friend of mine, asked me to attend a Women's Wellness Fair in Madison. I checked out all the different stations set up for various forms of wellness and alternative work being presented. I spoke to a lady who was teaching an emotional freedom technique called Tapping. During our conversation, I told her about my lower back pain and the reading of the cell memory prayer. I told her, "I don't understand what made me go back and re-read the cell memory prayer out loud."

She immediately interrupted me, "You know what made you do it, don't you?"

I replied, "No."

She stated, "It was your Spiritual Guide."

I mulled over these incidents, and had more questions than answers, *"Why am I experiencing vibrations and a humming sound? How did I know MaryAnn wanted a specific book? Was I supposed to read Sylvia Brown's books to learn the significance of the word "home" as it related to me? Did something happen to my lower back in a past life that carried over into this life and I was able to release it with prayer? Do I have a Spiritual Guide? Does it have a name?*

I was getting more deliberate nudges from either deep inside me or somewhere outside of me, like I had learned from the gentle nudges from the elm tree and *Awareness* in the confines of my constricted Cell. I was being told and shown things that were taking me outside of my box of conformity and comfort zone that will be difficult to explain. This couldn't be orchestrated just for me. This just doesn't happen, *does it?* The whirlwind of questions and the synchronistic events were picking up speed, and I was directly in the cross-hairs of the vortex.

❅ ❅ ❅ ❅ ❅

I surprised my friend MaryAnn with an early birthday gift by taking her to Milwaukee, to see the Mitchell Park Domes, the Milwaukee Museum, and ended the day with a surprise psychic reading for her with a renowned clairvoyant, and mystic from Mequon, named Beverly Kay.

After Beverly had completed MaryAnn's reading, she asked me, "Would you like to have a reading?" I wasn't planning on one, but we had enough time to fit it in before returning to Madison. Beverly advised me, "I will be recording your session. You can refer to it later on for accuracy." I had no idea what to expect. This was a first-time experience for me.

Beverly asked for my name and date of birth, and after doing some figuring on paper, she told me my numerology number was nine. She started the tape recorder and fired off in rapid succession things that meant absolutely nothing to me. (The actual recording is shown in italics.)

- *You are an A-Type person*
- *You are all things to all individuals—you are the salt of the earth with powers to influence the people you attract from all walks of life.*
- *Your mission in life is to help others*
- *25-7—Your numbers are very spiritual—it is a church*
- *You share not only yourself but your talents with the world*

- *You offer generously without expecting to receive in return*
- *Not bound by prejudice*
- *You are trusted by others because of your compassionate and broad-minded outlook*
- *You are ruled by your heart*
- *You have had your share of disappointments*
- *You have been through a lot of pain and suffering—life was not easy*
- *You are one tough, strong lady*
- *You have a heart of gold and will do just about anything for a friend*
- *You are a priest—really!*
- *You don't mean to hurt anyone, but you need the freedom to pursue your many interests*
- *You want to touch the hearts of many and would divulge your traits to anyone that you felt was genuinely interested*
- *In your desire to help it is important that you don't let people take advantage of you—you are very open*
- *You see the best in people—always the first to build a bridge over troubled waters—your theme is let there be peace on earth and let it begin with me*
- *Your welcome mat speaks many languages—from drop-in company to displaced relatives, there is always room for one more*
- *You have special friends of all walks of life*
- *You have strong emotions which can tear you apart if you let them*
- *Your home is your universe, it contains evidence you contribute to the community as a whole and want to travel*
- *You have talent for music or art—you have a need for harmony and beauty in your personal surroundings*

- *In fact, you can feel lovely anywhere in the world*
- *Marriage is stamped on your forehead—he will be a good man*
- *You have a sharp mind—don't hold back—you will not settle for just anyone*
- *New men and women coming into your life*
- *You will write, speak, lecture and have some fun*
- *You lay the foundation for your future—business and personal*

"I need to do a Rune card reading for you."
- *Card 1—You, your loved ones and possessions are protected by Heaven*
- *Card 2—Soulmate relationship—new romance with a spiritual base is here for you. The man who will be coming in is an accomplished person! He is worth waiting for.*

Having someone special in my life after the mastectomy was the furthest thing from my mind. Who would want to look at my disfigured body? I wasn't thrilled being told someone special would be coming into my life. I had been systematically putting those kinds of thoughts out of my mind as not being physically or emotionally possible for me.

- *Card 3—Working hard—take a nap and get some rest... timeout, timeout, timeout or you will burn out because a 25-7 needs timeouts!*
- *Card 4—Stay optimistic, your dreams are coming true*
- *Card 5—Don't quit right before the miracle occurs*
- *Card 6—Waves of prosperity, new abundance, and exciting opportunities wash over you now*

- *Card 7 — Have faith — your prayers are manifesting — remain confident and follow your guidance*

"Can I do an Angel Card reading for you?"

I sensed anxiousness in her request as if she hoped I wouldn't say no. I wondered if all her sessions involved all these various readings. None of this made any sense to me at all—Psychic Readings, Numerology, Rune cards, Angel cards, a future relationship, and she saw me as a priest— that's a hoot!

- *Relationship — huge thing — you are going into a business*
- *You are protected from all types of harm*
- *You are a very lucky woman*
- *There are a lot of angels and guides around you*
- *You are incredibly lucky — light a candle every day and thank God*
- *The worst is behind you — You need to relax and feel safe — you have a hard time doing that — you need to let go*
- *Keep charging ahead — don't take no for an answer*
- *Expect miraculous solutions to appear and they will — they will seem like magic, but it's not — it's Universal Law*
- *To help heal this situation — there will be a case coming up — see the other person's point of view with compassion*
- *The angel of marriage is assisting right now*
- *Know conditions are favorable right now. Wait or look into other options and ask the angels to help guide and comfort you. I take this as the business — the time isn't quite right…so wait a while.*
- *Yoga and exercise are essential for your spiritual growth now*

"WOW! You have one powerful mind."

- *You are flying high right now which may threaten other people but don't descend—don't come down—because others will soon become inspired by your examples—something is going to crank you up and turn you on, and you are going to GO!! Others are going to say look at her—who does she think she is—forget it—and go back to your center, and you will go up in consciousness*
- *Something active and new on the horizon—you just can't see it—take your time...take your time*

"I have a bag of Rune Stones. Do you feel up to me reading you with them?"

I agreed. What difference would one more thing I don't know anything about do for me?

Stone 1:
- *Simple prayer is a way of healing*
- *Ask through prayer what you want*
- *Be content to wait*
- *Journey—self-healing*
- *Regulate any excesses in your life*
- *Material advantage must not weigh heavy*
- *Feelings spontaneously expressed is the only right action now*
- *Take on your quest and continue on—you've been through hell—it's your time to live*

Stone 2:

- *Light a candle and say a prayer for your son. He's putting closure on things from his childhood that he can't understand himself*
- *Unseen powers are seen here*
- *Water*
- *Ebb and flow of nature*
- *Study spiritual matters for transformation*

Stone 3:

- *Possession*
- *Fulfillment*
- *Nourishment from the world and Divine*
- *Enjoy your good fortune and share it with others*

Stone 4:

- *Fruit bearing branch*
- *Shift has occurred*
- *Blessings in emotion and knowledge*
- *Carried across to tell by the Holy Spirit*
- *Soul illuminated from within*

Stone 5:

- *Submit and be still*
- *Surrender to display courage*
- *Pulsing of unwanted forces*
- *Freeing the forces*

*"Men would kill for your numbers...8 = business, 7 = marriage, 6 = healing/teacher. You should get angel cards and read them. Get the book titled **Super Beings** by John Price. Can you take off the necklace you are wearing so I can hold it?"*

I thought it was a strange request, but I unlatched it and handed it to her. I watched her hold it in the palm of her left hand and cover it with her right hand as she looked directly at me across the desk that divided us. She was using everything in her professional arsenal to read me, and I was uncomfortable and exhausted by it all.

Time today was supposed to be for MaryAnn, not for me. I should have said no when Beverly asked if I wanted a reading. All her psychic reading sessions were arranged by appointment only. Why had she asked if I wanted one?

- *You will get married*
- *Total transformation and rebirth before new person evolves in your life*
- *You have 22-4 for the rest of your life*
- *More and more psychic and clairvoyant*
- *You are very sensitive*
- *You are grounded — won't become a space cadet*
- *Three Lessons: Father and husbands — Father = Good*
- *Standing today on your own — patent it — money in it*
- *As a little girl, you were shy and timid*
- *7 = reserved — now you found your mouth — part of time to be alone*
- *2 = nerves around stomach — you won't eat*
- *8 = business*

Beverly handed the necklace back to me and leaned forward on the desk that was separating us. She looked directly at me as if she had something paramount to tell me. There was a long pause and then she continued to read me without any gadgets.

- *You have no knowledge of this…you are on a spiritual journey*
- *You are in tune with metaphysics*
- *When you meet the man coming into your life…he will have been in the sciences, married and divorced. Wife hurt him badly. He doesn't want anything to do with marriage. He will fall in love with you first.*
- *When you look him in the eye, you will feel a current from your head to your toes, and you will know*
- *He will be good-looking—also a businessman—light gray in hair—has a strong spiritual background*
- *You wrote him down in your book of life—no doubt he is coming*
- *Relax and unwind*
- *Start to journal—very important*
- *You have power*
- *You will see all these things come to pass*

The reading ended, and Beverly stood up and stepped out from behind her desk. She stood in front of me and took both my hands in hers and said, *"You are a very special person. I'm so glad you came to see me."* She turned off the recording machine and handed me the tape.

When I arrived home, I tossed the tape into a catch-all box on my work desk and forgot about it, completely unaware of its telling, impending significance.

❈ ❈ ❈ ❈

"Trust in the Lord with all your heart, and lean not on your own understanding.

In all your ways acknowledge Him, and he shall direct your paths."
—Proverbs 3:5 NKJV

Chapter Four
See-e-e-sters

*"The friend who can be silent with us in a moment of despair
or confusion, who can stay with us in an hour of grief and
bereavement, who can tolerate not knowing...not healing,
not curing...that is a friend who cares."*
—Henri Nouwen

With my health improving, I moved to a new place of employment that brought me closer to home and offered me more challenge. After a year with the company, a senior manager approached me and asked if I would mentor a new assistant coming onboard in her department, Darcy Lutzow. The company had an office manager who handled the mentoring of all new employees, but for some unknown reason to me, the senior manager wanted to circumvent her. I agreed to help if my boss approved and he did.

Darcy had a commanding presence. She stood six feet tall, with long dark hair, a beautiful smile, and green eyes that danced with mischief. Her laughter was contagious for all who heard it, and it became her signature card. Our friendship grew with time, and she became my surrogate sister. Someone to share things with and know we had each other's back. We golfed, learned Spanish, cried through her divorce, laughed our way through Ireland, and celebrated when she found Kurt Pederson, a man who loved her for all her beautiful qualities. Darcy often referred to us as *See-e-e-sters,* and I affectionately referred to her as the Social Director, because she was great at planning events for our shared circle of friends at work.

Heaven had indeed sent me an earthly guardian angel who served as a wall of protection around me at a time when I needed it most in my still-fragile, recovering state of being. Unknown to her, Darcy helped me to trust myself and rejoin the world of the living. To hear her laughter put a smile on my face, and lifted my soul, and anyone else's who was within hearing distance, without even knowing what she was laughing about.

Then there was the hug—there was no escaping it. Darcy never let anyone leave a social event without extending her elongated arms out like a fisherman casting his net into the ocean for his daily catch of fish. No one could escape Darcy's arms without getting a gentle bear hug to say goodbye and send them on their way. Darcy's heart was a bright beacon of light, and she cared about everyone she met.

After the mastectomy, I was very self-conscious about my surgical disfigurement and thought I would never be touched or loved by a man. I was living the life of a nun and hiding my wounded body. How does one present oneself as a Picasso painting with a disfigurement to someone special and hope that person would be able to look past the scars and only see what was in one's heart? In the beginning, Darcy's demanding hugs were awkward for me, but with time, she taught me I deserved to be touched and shown love. I learned to ease into the hugs with gratitude for her persistence, and I discovered the beauty of returning a hug to her and sharing hugs with others I knew.

The unusual request to mentor Darcy introduced me to my BFF (best friend forever).

※ ※ ※ ※ ※

Summer was quickly drifting away, and the thought of another Wisconsin winter just a few months off was reason enough for Darcy to plan a getaway weekend in July at a resort in Mishicot, Wisconsin. Reservations had been confirmed for our Friday night arrival and our early Saturday morning tee time on the resort's 27-hole golf course. As an added bonus, the resort was featuring a Country Western themed weekend with live music we both enjoyed.

We left work early to beat the heavy vacation traffic heading to northern Wisconsin. With the front seat of the car pushed back as far as it would go, Darcy's knees were tight up against the dashboard for the entire two-and-a-half-hour ride in my Chevy Prism. Upon exiting the car at the resort, her back started giving her problems. We unpacked the car, set up our room and headed back down the road to a local establishment for a traditional Wisconsin Friday night fish fry. I watched Darcy struggle to get back into the car after dinner and knew she would not be able to golf with her back problem. The hotel brochure resting on the car dashboard showed a spa service available to all guests, so we hurried back to the resort to see if she could get in before it closed.

Darcy tried to hide her discomfort and kept saying, "I'll be alright in the morning to golf."

I told her, "I won't golf with you. You'll end up in the hospital the way you are right now."

We arrived at the spa, and the person working inside told us she was closing up for the evening. I asked if there were any openings first thing in the morning to help Darcy. The attendant introduced herself as Barb Krull, and she checked the appointment book. They were totally booked. Barb said, "I'm off tomorrow until 4:00 p.m. I would be happy to come in from Green Bay and take care of Darcy in the morning." Darcy picked 9:30 a.m. for her one-hour deep-tissue massage. Barb then turned to me and asked, "And what would you like?"

I didn't expect to have anything done. With golf out of the question for Saturday morning, I asked for a pedicure.

Barb replied, "We don't do pedicures; we only do massages."

I told Barb, "I had a massage a few years earlier, and my body hurt for two days. I don't want a repeat performance, so I'll pass."

Barb asked, "Would you like to try a hot-stone massage?" I had never had one, and after she explained the use of the hot stones, I agreed to a 30-minute half-body session following Darcy's appointment the next morning.

Saturday morning we headed down to the spa. Darcy was limping more than ever, and the decision not to golf was justified. I read a book while I waited in the waiting room as Darcy was getting some well-needed relief. At 10:30 a.m. Barb came up to me in the waiting room and bent down, so her face was directly in front of mine and quietly remarked, "You are such a special friend. Darcy will be out shortly. I'm going to prepare the room for your hot-stone massage and will be back to get you." As she walked away, I wondered what she meant saying "I was such a special friend?" Were they talking about me during Darcy's session?

Barb came back to get me at the same time Darcy arrived in the waiting room. I told Darcy, "I'll meet you in the pool area in thirty minutes."

Darcy replied, "I'm going to use the whirlpool while I wait."

In the massage room, the lighting was dim and it gave the room a feeling of softness and tranquility; typical spa music was playing in the background. I lay face down on the massage table and readied myself for some weekend pampering. I heard Barb taking deep breaths and releasing them as I listened to the clinking of stones she was working with. I hoped this type of massage would be gentle for me. Since experiencing cancer, my body had become more sensitive than usual. As the massage proceeded, we casually talked while Barb placed the hot stones on my body.

I mentioned I was taking a yoga class and it wasn't very comfortable for my body. Barb replied, "Yoga is good, but you can achieve the same results in other ways through meditation." (*Click 1—Note to Kathy: "Meditation" is used in religious practices.*)

I replied, "I've never meditated."

I shared with Barb, "I have a friend who smells carnations when people pass away, and she's trying to figure out why it is happening to her."

Barb responded, "I don't envy your friend for the gift she has. She should see someone to help her deal with it. She might want to work in a hospice setting to help people transition." (*Click 2—Note to Kathy: She used the word "gift," which is another term used in psychic references.*)

I was swimming in uncharted waters with this conversation, and I didn't know enough about "meditation" or "gifts" other than what I had already read in the two Sylvia Brown books and what little had been learned from my friend MaryAnn.

I asked, "Who should she see?"

Barb replied, "I know an excellent guide." (*Click 3 — Note to Kathy: She used the word "guide," another term used in religious references.*) Three key references were given and the third time is always a charm in my book.

I asked Barb a question I had never asked anyone before, "Do you have a gift?"

There was an awkward pause as Barb continued to place the hot stones on my body. I thought, *"Did I go too far asking the question?"* I knew I was in unfamiliar territory, but my gut told me it was the right question to ask. Barb responded in a soft tone of voice, "I will say this to you...I do massage, and I work with energy."

I took a stab in the dark and asked, "Do you see auras around people?"

She replied, "No, but you will know what it is before you leave here today." I had no clue what I would know about energy before I left. I stopped asking questions.

Barb softly remarked, "You know you came to see me today for a reason."

With a smidgeon of a laugh, I replied, "No, I thought I would be on the golf course early this morning."

Barb asked, "Do you realize people pass through our lives for a reason?"

I replied, "Yes, I became very aware of it when I met a young emergency room doctor and his wife while dealing with cancer. I'm sensitive to it and often share what happened between us with others."

Barb asked, "Do you realize these people don't always stay?" I replied, "Yes."

Barb then told me, "Your friend Darcy is experiencing more pain than what she came to see me about today." I was struck speechless and didn't know where this conversation was headed. A part of me wanted to ask about Darcy's unknown pain, but I thought curiosity kills the cat. If Darcy wanted to tell me something, she would in her own time, so I stayed quiet. It was as if my subconscious was telling me, *"You don't need to know."* The room remained silent, and Barb continued with the hot-stone massage for the remaining time.

I was so relaxed when the half-hour session was finished. For the first time in years, I didn't feel any discomfort in my body. I had learned to live with my pain due to being so sensitive, but this was a small piece of heaven to be pain-free. I asked, "If you don't have another appointment after mine, could you upgrade my half-body session to a full-body?"

She responded, "Yes, I only came in to take care of Darcy and you today." Barb then asked me to turn over on my back for the next thirty minutes. I was glad I was able to extend my appointment, and with my eyes closed, I continued to be pain-free and tranquil.

Barb stood behind my head, reached down to the middle of my back and then slowly pulled her hand out along my spine. As her hand moved up onto the back of my head, I began to see a circle appear in front of me of the most beautiful, bright electric-green and another color encircled it of bright electric purple. The colors pulsated simultaneously to the sound of a mother's heartbeat in a baby's womb, and they enlarged outwardly with each pulsing beat. The heartbeat wasn't mine, but was another coming from outside of me. I did not want to open my eyes and let go of the beautiful colors displayed in front of me. They were so bright I wondered if someone had turned on an overhead light in the room. I waved my hand over my face area to see if I could see the shadow of my hand moving over my closed eyes and I couldn't.

The pulsing colors started to go out beyond my peripheral vision, and for a brief second, I was frightened of the unknown. I didn't think I would be able to stay with the event unfolding in front of me. My curiosity about the beauty I was observing quickly outweighed my fear, and my body released, and the soothing heartbeat embraced me. I was instantly floating in another space and time as a voyeur observing the beauty of the rings of color from a distance as they continued to expand in size to the heartbeat encompassing everything.

My presence was no larger than a fleck of dust compared to the scale of the circles of color, and they were small in comparison to the vast Universe extending out beyond them of planets, galaxies, and stars. The colors were soothing like a mother's voice to a newborn and at the same time, mystical. The green circle emitted unconditional love and forgiveness that comes from the heart. The purple circle encompassing the green circle epitomized a higher power and presence. The heartbeat was a field of energy acting as a bridge that connected everything between our world within and the world that is outside of us.

I was completely aware of being in two places at one time. I became a conduit between the two worlds. One foot was here on earth in the room lying on a massage table with Barb, and the other was somewhere else in between. I was shown a simple truth of the Universe of how we are all connected simultaneously as one by love, compassion and by something much greater than all of us that emits energy. I wasn't handed a book to read to understand it, and I wasn't told in spoken words. All I can say is it was an immediate knowing from deep within.

Continuing to keep my eyes closed, I told Barb, "I'm seeing the most beautiful green and purple colors pulsing in front of me." When I acknowledged verbally what I was experiencing, warm tears cascaded down both sides of my face, and my body started to tremble and came back to the massage room. I opened my eyes. I had slipped from one dimension back to another as effortlessly as taking in a breath of fresh air. *Is this what it is like to take our last breath on earth? How beautiful and easy it was to let go.* The mystery and fear associated with death had been eradicated from my being.

Barb quietly whispered into my right ear, "That's the energy I told you about." Barb came along the right side of the massage table and touched my elbow, "I don't have to talk to you about the problems you are having and the sadness in your heart because I work from the heart." She moved her hand down my right arm to my fingers, and said, "You are just beginning your journey." She turned and walked out of the room. It took me a moment to absorb what had just happened before I could even think about getting dressed.

I walked out into the waiting room, and Darcy was just coming through the door from the whirlpool area. She stood statuesque in the doorway with her hands on her hips and in a bold and questioning voice, asked, "Where the hell have you been? What happened to you?" I wondered the same thing and then realized my half-hour appointment had turned into an hour and Darcy hadn't been informed of the change of plans. It was unfortunate I had to make her wait and turn into a wrinkled prune from her additional whirlpool time. "Darcy, you aren't going to believe what just happened to me."

Barb stood off to the side behind a glass enclosure where her co-workers congregated. I walked over and reached through the glass opening to shake her hand, and she responded, "No, I'll come out and give you a hug." Barb hugged me tightly, and as I watched her turn and walk back behind the glassed enclosure, I looked at her and thought there was something angelic about her. She had straight blonde hair, no makeup, was dressed all in white and had no additional color added to her outfit. Her voice was soft spoken and shy-mannered. *Was she an earth angel sent to give me a message?* I couldn't discuss this with anyone. They'd call the men in white jackets to come and get me.

I quietly asked her, "Why did I see colors?"

Barb smiled and gently replied, "You need to see a Reiki person." Reiki was an entirely foreign word to me. I wanted to ask more questions, and I knew I'd kick myself later for not pursuing it. It just wasn't the time or place with others standing around. I knew this was going to be the beginning of my journey to search for answers to things I needed to know more about.

As Darcy and I walked back to our room, my mind reeled from what had just happened. I questioned Darcy, "Did you talk about me during your session with Barb?"

Darcy replied, "No, we only talked about my back problem, where I was from and small talk."

My "Doubting Thomas" pattern didn't believe Darcy's response. There had to be a reason Barb said I was such a special friend.

When we got into our hotel room, I told Darcy, "Barb told me you were in a lot of pain and not the pain you came to see her about today." Suddenly, Darcy let out a wail that came from a cavernous place within her. It was an exclamation of deep pain I had never heard, and it startled me.

She released a watershed of tears from deep within her. She blurted out, "My father beat my mother and gave us kids gifts to make up for it." Darcy continued to repeat, with tears continuing to stream down her face, "It wasn't right! It wasn't right!" I was shocked at her immediate, honest and raw response. It was definitely something Darcy needed to let out. I stood in silence across the room and wondered how Barb had known Darcy was experiencing more pain than in her back? How had Barb known about the sadness in my heart?

Darcy and I went to lunch. I wanted so badly to talk to her about the recent events I had been experiencing before our weekend trip, and hopefully be able to explain to her intelligibly what all happened during the hot-stone massage without her thinking I lost touch with reality. She experienced something with my message to her from Barb, and I hoped she would be open to listening to what I had to tell her since she would be the first person I would share it all with.

I started to go through the litany of things I had experienced, and Darcy remained quiet through it all. I told her, "I can't explain it. I didn't ask for this, but something is happening to me." She continued to remain quiet, and the good friend and *See-e-e-ster* she was, she didn't take off running. We dropped the subject for the remainder of the afternoon.

After dinner, we attended the live Western band performance. People staying at the hotel came prepared to look the part for the evening's event with Western boots, blue jeans, Western-cut shirts, and cowboy hats to top off their wardrobe. The event had a drawing for two free tickets to a County Music Jamboree event coming up in September. The drawing was scheduled to be announced when the band took their first break.

Darcy questioned, "Should I fill out the entry form? Kurt and I would enjoy this."

I replied, "Absolutely, you're going to win."

Darcy ignored my response and filled out the entry form and put it in the barrel with those of the other guests hoping to win. At intermission, the leader of the band pulled out the winning entry form and announced Darcy's name.

Darcy looked across the table at me, "How did you know I would win?"

With everything we experienced that morning and talked about at lunch, we both looked at each other and cracked up laughing.

✻ ✻ ✻ ✻ ✻

I still felt uneasy on Sunday about my hot-stone massage experience. I was anxious to get home and see if I could get in touch with MaryAnn and tell her what Barb said about her, and ask if she could help me understand what happened to me.

MaryAnn was home when I called and invited me to come over. It was a warm summer evening, and I was glad MaryAnn wanted to sit out on her patio. I didn't want her husband Gary to hear our conversation when I talked to her about my amazing weekend experience. MaryAnn giggled when I finished telling her all the details and said, "You were opened up."

Confused by her response, I asked, "What do you mean?"

She responded in a way that was as ordinary as requesting a glass of water, "You were able to connect with the spiritual side." I still didn't understand enough about what was going on to feel comfortable with her short, concise and "it happens every day" response. I needed more concrete information. The "Doubting Thomas" within me was rising to the surface. I needed to understand and have a logical explanation of what happened to me.

I shared with MaryAnn what Barb said about her needing to seek out an excellent guide and possibly think about working with hospice patients to help their transition with her gifts. MaryAnn's eyes started tearing up, and the tears started running down her cheeks as she sat quietly taking in what I had told her.

"Barb said she knows an excellent guide, but I didn't think to ask who it was. I was too dumbstruck by all that happened."

MaryAnn asked, "Could you contact Barb and find out who I should see? I'd also like to schedule a hot-stone massage with her."

I agreed to contact Barb about the guide information, but I waited a week before I called. With all that had happened, I wondered if Barb would actually be there when I called, especially since I thought there was something angelic about her. What if I called the spa and they told me she didn't work there? I would lose it.

After a few anxious inquiries from MaryAnn during the week asking if I had reached out to Barb, I finally got up the courage to call her on Saturday afternoon. Barb was working and offered to call me on Sunday so we would have more time to talk.

Barb called back and laughed when I told her about my thoughts of her possibly being an angel when I had looked at her. I spoke to her about the keywords that came up in our conversation during the massage and how they clicked for me to ask if she had a gift.

Barb remarked, "You're asking me if I had a gift was an affirmation for me from you."

She gave me the name of the guide MaryAnn wanted. The guide's name was Donna Marie Levy.

Barb said, "We'll be in touch with each other."

I told her, "My friend MaryAnn would like to schedule a hot-stone massage with you."

Barb replied firmly, "Your friend isn't meant to meet me. She needs to see the guide. What happened to you had nothing to do with the hot-stone massage. You were open to accepting the energy healing. If someone isn't open to it, I could get hurt."

Barb told me she had gone to the guide, Donna Marie, and the guide saw a rainbow of colors around her.

I questioned, "What does that mean?" Barb got out a book titled *Chakra Clearing* by Doreen Virtue and told me it's a symbol of an energy healer and a star traveler.

I asked, "What is a star traveler?"

Barb replied, "That's a whole other area, but it means it is someone who is on the earth for the first time and is an energy healer." Barb then told me the meaning of the colors I had seen, and she recommended I get a copy of the book. Barb shared with me the definitions in the book of what the colors I had seen represented.

- *"Electric Green: A healer (may be a professional healer, a natural healer, or one who is unaware of his or her healing abilities). Also, indicates that prayers for own healing are working. Working with Archangel Raphael.*
- *Electric Purple: In tune with the Divine spiritual realm; enlightenment, and claircognizance."*

My "Doubting Thomas" pattern was resurfacing, and I just had to ask Barb directly if Darcy had talked about me during her massage session. I hoped Barb would be able to fill me in on more conversation between her and Darcy so I could get an answer to the "special friend" comment.

Barb confirmed, "We did not discuss you other than Darcy mentioned you were very sensitive and you might not be able to tolerate the hot stones." My "Doubting Thomas" was put back in its box.

When I finished talking to Barb, I had received answers to some things, but was left with more lingering questions. *How do you meditate? Am I healer? Do I work with angels?* I need to look up the word claircognizance for a precise definition and see if it fits me.

Barb wasn't an angel, but she was the next best thing to experiencing one. I spent time researching books about star travelers and their traits, and Barb fit the description to a tee. I also purchased the *Chakra Clearing* book.

Experiencing energy through colors was my next-level kick-off point. The soft nudges had ended, and now the wake-up slaps and cold water in the face to pay attention had begun. The Divine was opening up my world to new possibilities, realities, thoughts of life beyond, and the beauty it has to share with everyone.

ꘜ ꘜ ꘜ ꘜ ꘜ

"Be still, and know that I am God."
—Psalm 46:10 NIV

CHAPTER FIVE
VISIONS AND MESSAGES

"What was said to the rose to make it open
was said to me here in my heart when I met you."
—Rumi

The bright colors of purple and green continued to display themselves whenever I closed my eyes. They would come in quick flashes or like dancing blobs in a 1960's lava lamp, and increased in size until they filled my entire field of vision. I watched the blobs drift with ease and beauty, and then expand and contract like seasoned contemporary dancers. It left me enjoying these encounters in a peaceful space of *Now*.

❦ ❦ ❦ ❦ ❦

Taking some quiet time for myself, I decided to stay in my bedroom and catch up on the early Sunday morning news programs. I jumped out of bed and retrieved the morning newspaper from the front doorstep, and climbed back into bed to enjoy both news media vehicles before anyone else needed me for the day.

I briefly perused the newspaper headlines and put the paper down on my lap so I could look up at the television. A bright green blob floated in front of me and beautifully turned into the shape of a heart. A bright purple blob appeared next to it, and it too transformed into the form of a heart. Both hearts slowly pulsed and drifted toward me and remained suspended in front of me as I watched them in total wonder.

Watching the blobs turn into hearts reminded me of my childhood days when I would lie down in the warm summer grass and watch white cumulus clouds. I would cloud scry, and watch as the clouds shifted into animals and faces as they moved across the richly colored blue sky.

The two hearts had profound significance because tears ran down my face as I watched them. I just didn't know what it meant for me at this time. This was the first time I experienced an event with my eyes open and being entirely in actual time. Where was this coming from? It's the same effect as when you buy a 1000-piece puzzle, and you can't finish it because not all the pieces are in the box.

While making breakfast, I shared my morning experience with Mom. I was able to convey to her what had been happening to me, and she listened with genuine interest. She wasn't able to shed any motherly advice about what was going on or tell me she had any similar situations in her lifetime. She didn't make me feel uncomfortable sharing everything with her, so she continued to be a protective shelter I could go to and know all would be okay to confide in her.

✄ ✄ ✄ ✄ ✄

A month later, two vivid dreams were shown to me during the early morning hours. They weren't the kind of dreams I usually had at night, and by the time I took my morning shower, I couldn't remember what I had dreamt about.

These dreams were explicit, and the details were vibrant and precise. An indelible ink pen was painting it all in my memory for future reference, never to be forgotten.

I was in a classroom with a lot of people, and the colors of everyone's clothing were brilliant. I only knew one person, my friend MaryAnn, and she sat in the first seat of my row, and I was seated in the last chair. I never saw MaryAnn's face, only the back of her, but I knew it was her. All the others in the room were unknown to me.

A man stood behind a tall, bright, white stone table, and was teaching the class. He was tall, had a weathered, handsome face and beautiful gray hair. He wore a white shirt with a Nehru collar and black dress pants. The teacher came out from behind the white stone table and approached me. When he stood beside me, all the people in the room were gone, and he embraced me.

The second dream was shown to me in black and white. It looked like an artist had used compressed charcoal sticks to paint the individual pictures on bright white canvas.

People came toward me looking like they were from biblical times with long hair, beards and wearing clothing from that era, while many others looked like Native American Indians. They appeared and disappeared in front of me as fast as one could click a television remote. I wished they would slow down so I could have had a more detailed look at each of them, but I had no control over them making their presence known to me. The only thing consistent with all of them was the beauty of their eyes that gave me a brief glimpse into their hearts as they quickly passed by me.

The importance of the dreams coming to me in color or black and white had started to mean something to me. The colored visions represented a future event, and the black-and-white images meant something that had already happened. I was apparently tapping into a visual field of information from somewhere, and it was exciting to take it all in, but I wished I had those few missing puzzle pieces so I could see the whole picture.

✖ ✖ ✖ ✖ ✖

The green and purple colors continued during the day and at night for the next few months.

On a Sunday morning around 3:00 a.m., I woke up to my dad's voice clearly calling loudly for Mom. I jumped out of bed to respond because it sounded so clear and close like Dad was right outside my bedroom door. I opened the door, and he wasn't there, and the house was dark. The only light to be seen was the moonlight shining through the dining room skylight.

I proceeded to walk through the house to see if there was a light on under Dad's bedroom door—nothing. I went to the sunroom where Dad liked to sit in his favorite chair during the day, to see if he was seated in the dark—he wasn't there.

I decided to go back to bed.

I joined Mom in the kitchen for breakfast. Dad was sleeping later than usual, so I told Mom what I had heard and done during the early morning hours. Dad got up and did not come to the kitchen like he always did for his breakfast. He went and sat down in his favorite chair on the sun porch. He was staring out the window as though he were in deep thought.

Mom and I were concerned, so we walked out to the sun porch to see if he was ok. I asked, "Dad, did you have a good night's rest?"

He replied, in a grumpy and agitated voice, "No!"

I asked, "Why not?"

He replied, "I dreamt I was at a track meet."

I laughed and asked him, "What were you doing at a track meet?"

He replied in a troubled and concerned voice, "I was calling for your mother."

Mom's mouth dropped wide open, and we both looked at each other in surprise. I was thankful I had shared my experience with her before Dad got up. Mom's reaction was an affirmation from her to me that something was definitely going on and she was able to confirm it with me. She eagerly waited for me to share more experiences with her.

❧❧❧❧❧

The events had been gentle and easy to accept until two unusual circumstances left me dumbfounded, frightened and not sure where to turn for help.

*I turned on a music CD, titled **Perfect Balance** so I could listen to it when I went to bed for the night. With eyes closed, I listened to the music and then heard a gentle flapping sound, like a bird's wings, next to my left ear. I opened my eyes, and the sound stopped. I thought it strange.*

I closed my eyes and continued to listen to the CD. The flapping sound returned with a considerable force of energy. I was swiftly lifted up and off the bed and suspended in midair with my arms outstretched at the foot of the bed. I was slowly turned in midair, and looked down at the bed—it was empty. My body was quickly projected sideways through the wall of the bedroom to the outside of the house. I was again turned so I could look back into the house. My body returned to the bedroom and was gently placed on the bed. I opened my eyes, and my favorite song was playing on the CD titled—7th Chakra—Be Still and Know That I Am.

Two days later the second unusual event occurred.

I opened my eyes during the early morning hours and saw the outline of my hands and arms going out of my body in an upward direction. I could see an outline of bright shimmering white light, of small stars vibrating and holding together the shape of my fingers, palms, and arms, with nothing inside of the outlines. I tried to lift myself off the bed to go with them, but I was pushed back down onto the bed with a substantial force and fell back to sleep.

When I woke up, my entire body was vibrating harder than I had ever experienced before, and whatever I saw going out was returning into my body.

What am I being shown? Did my soul take a vacation? Where did I go? These two events were more than my mind could comprehend. I was shaken to the core of my being by both events and had no natural explanation for what had happened.

I stopped listening to music and reading books until I could talk to someone who could guide me through this. I wasn't able to share these two events with Mom—at least not yet.

❧ ❧ ❧ ❧ ❧

Barb, the massage therapist, had said she knew an excellent guide. I hoped she was right because I pursued the guide, Donna Marie Levy, to see if she could help me to understand what was happening and how to handle it. Information on the Internet stated Donna Marie was an ordained ministerial counselor, clairvoyant and she channeled messages from Spirit and the Akashic records.

I arranged a reading at Donna Marie's home in Green Bay, Wisconsin. I had told Mom a few days earlier I was going to have a psychic reading, but I didn't say why. She was just anxious for me to return and share everything with her.

I prepared to leave the house early on Saturday morning before Mom or Dad got up. As I opened the door from the kitchen to the garage, I heard Dad say, "Where are you going at this time of the morning?" I quickly turned around, and Dad was standing at the entrance to the kitchen. Busted!

Dad never gets up this early in the morning, and I had not shared with him what was going on as I did with Mom. Call it a sixth sense; I just knew he would not understand, without my going into great detail, and I did not have the time or the desire to have him dismiss me. This was something stronger than I could explain, and I needed to go. Nothing was going to stop me. I replied, "Dad, I can't tell you right now. We'll talk when I get home."

❧ ❧ ❧ ❧ ❧

Donna Marie and I sat together in her healing room, filled with bright golden sunshine that created an atmosphere of warmth and calm. All the furniture was white wicker, and the walls were painted in soft, muted tones. A massage table stood off to the right of us. The room was spacious, and everything was placed to give a feeling of feng shui and a flow of balanced energy.

Donna Marie stated, "I will record the reading for your reference at a later time.

"This reading will make more sense in the future than it does today. Full life and capabilities and your direction are in here if only between the lines. There will be the direction of abilities and how you present them to the world.

Before I lose this picture, I see you driving a car, and no one else is with you. I see this as you'll be in charge of your life. I believe it's how you'll feel whether you have a partner or not. The car is quite nice, and you drive up a horseshoe-shaped driveway to a beautiful house on a large property. There is a lake behind the house. It is a peaceful place with a wooded area to the right, and animals are looking out towards the house. I see this house as a mansion. The house is quite extended. It's more ranch style, and it goes off into the distance and always has new rooms being added."

I giggled and made a flippant remark, "Maybe my ship will finally come in, and life will be great."

Donna Marie's voice changed, and she looked directly at me and quickly informed me, "No, it is the house you are building on the other side from what you will be doing on the earth." She then looked off to the right of me and said, "I see this house as a mansion of your soul. I see this as soul growth for you. What is gorgeous about this house is it's made of pink bricks, and they shine back at me as I'm looking at it. There are diamonds in each brick. Each brick has its own light coming from it, and I know each block placed in the house was done yourself with your own heart's intentions, as you continue to build the house. There is great serenity there.

If you are not a nurse, you should be. Have you gone into the medical profession?"

I replied, "Years ago I wanted to be a nurse, but because of a lower back problem, I did not pursue it."

Donna Marie responded, "You might do it differently. You are a healer.

Did you lose someone a few years back? Did someone move away from you? When I come to your heart, there is a feeling of space—emptiness. What is his name?"

I replied, "My son."

"You have one sister. There is a young married man around her."

I replied, "Not that I'm aware of. She's married. Could it be my son? They were close through the years, like brother and sister. He has been away from all of us."

Donna Marie replied, "Why do I feel he's ashamed? He won't look at me. He's ashamed of something, and he has to get over the shame and go to the core of himself to where the good is. Your sister and son really need to talk. They need to be connected in some way. They've both taken on quite a lifetime to overcome many things. Why do I want to say he can't forgive himself? If he's projecting it out to other *people instead, then he's not looking at it responsibly. What I see with him is he is blaming himself—shame—regretful for something he might have done or something he's been judged for. He needs to get past it and move on and be strong. Why do I see walls around him? Is he in prison?"*

I replied, "No, but he is a police officer."

Donna Marie asked, "Does he go into prisons?"

I replied, "I don't know."

Donna Marie stated, "There are walls around him. Does he put the barricade up around himself? Knowing your son, does this sound like him?"

I replied, "Yes, if you mean walls within him."

"Your Heavenly Council consists of many ascended masters sitting together and looking down on me. Moses, Abraham, and Melchizedek are just a few, and there are many heads of Indian tribes. You have walked the earth before with Melchizedek. You were a priest. The Council states you have done what you were sent to do on the Earth Plane, and now you are moving into the spiritual side of your life. You will be able to say what other people cannot say.

"You are an astro traveler, and you are able to project yourself out of the body.

"You are going to acquire a piece of jewelry; it will be futuristic. You will come in contact with a stone, and it begins with the letter T. It's called tanzanite. When this happens, you will know you are ready. There are techniques you have not yet encountered, and they have not yet come to the earth that you will do. You will understand quantum physics and the meaning of Pi (π).

"I see two white doves flying together, and they are carrying a bright white piece of material between their beaks.

I have never seen this sign before. I'm not sure what it means. It could be a personal union like a marriage planned before you came to the earth or it may be a message you will bring to the world. Remember what I'm telling you. It will make sense when it happens.

"Don't be frightened by what you are experiencing. There will be more coming to you. Make sure you start to journal your experiences. When they happen, you will be able to refer back and confirm your messages."

The reading ended, and I asked Donna Marie, "Can I talk to you about some vivid dreams and recent experiences that have left me unraveled? It's really why I came to see you today."

She replied, "Yes."

I began my litany of events. I shared with Donna Marie how fast the biblical and Native Indian faces came at me, and stated, "I wished I could have had more time to get a more detailed look at them."

She replied, "You are clairvoyant. The next time something like that happens, ask them to slow down."

I told her about hearing Dad calling for Mom.

She replied, "You heard him because you were able to be in his dream. You astro-travel, and you are clairaudient."

I explained to her about the vibrations and humming sounds and picking books unique to someone without my knowing how or why.

She replied, "You are claircognizant and precognitive."

I saved the unusual and hard-to-talk-about events until last. It would be hard to tell Donna Marie, but I needed to know. I shared with her my experience of being lifted up and going through the wall of our house and back in. I explained to her how I was able to see an outline of bright, shimmering, miniature stars of my hands, palms, and arms going out of my body in an upward direction and the return of the same into my body.

She replied, "Don't be frightened, you are being shown something you have forgotten. You already experienced something momentous, and there will be more things like this coming to you."

I shared with her the energy event when I had the hot-stone massage, and she replied, "That was your beginning. You need to journal your events. They will be significant for you."

I looked in the direction of the massage table and asked Donna Marie, "Do you do massage work?"

She replied, "No, I teach and do Reiki." I swallowed hard when she said Reiki, remembering what Barb, the massage therapist, told me: *"You need to see a Reiki person."*

I asked Donna Marie, "Do you have any classes starting up that I could get into to learn Reiki?"

She enrolled me in her next session of classes two months out.

✂ ✂ ✂ ✂ ✂

I approached Dad when I returned home and asked, "Dad, do you have time to sit down so I can talk to you about where I went so early this morning?"

He replied curtly and in his usual dismissive tone, "I don't want to know anything about it."

What I had sensed before leaving the house was correct. It was better I didn't share my events with him. I was on a journey, and the wind was blowing me in a direction that would not be comfortable for him to accept—not at this time.

I listened to Donna Marie's tape recording again before going to bed. I was amazed she knew I had one sister and her accurate description of my son. I had not mentioned either of them to her before the reading. Donna Marie sensed the empty space in my heart regarding my son, just like Barb had sensed the sadness and Beverly had asked me to pray for my son for things he is dealing with.

Donna Marie had no idea I had a Native Indian background, at least not from me, and I realized the faces I had seen before going to see her were those of the Heavenly Council she described to me. My being able to astro-travel was another surprise since I hadn't told her anything about my events until after she completed my reading.

How does someone come up with these things without knowing me at all? Going over the tape recording, I realized I needed to experience this to understand that more things are going on in the unseen world around all of us than I ever realized. I needed to hear these affirmations to become sensitive, aware, and open to them because more would be coming. *Mom is going to love this.*

I returned to the bookstore to purchase a writing journal and to find another book to try and learn more about my experiences. As I perused the shelves with my hands running across the book spines, I stopped when I touched the book *Awakening the Mystic Gift* by Jane Doherty. My fingers told me to stop, and my body followed suit with the vibration and humming sound like all the times before. I would not ignore the message I was getting. I knew I was being guided and I was surrendering to it and trusting where it would lead me.

I started to read the book after dinner and continued reading it when I went to bed. I could not put the book down. The story of my life and the author were crossing each other. Jane Doherty had her "Doubting Thomas" questions about what was happening to her and her constant searching for answers. The book helped me to know I wasn't alone on my journey. Someone else had been on the same boat heading into the unknown mist.

I finished reading the book around 2:30 a.m. and had to be up in three and a half hours to get ready for work. I quickly dropped off to sleep and was shown two more vivid visions.

In the distance, I could see a right-angle corner of a room with a shelf on the wall. I could see lots of colors blurred together on top of the shelf, but I could not make out what was on it. I remembered what Donna Marie told me, so I asked, "Come closer please." The vision moved toward me at hyperspeed. It was so close I couldn't make anything out. It was a huge blob of colors all mixed together in front of my face. I then asked, "Can you move it back just a little, please?" It shifted away from me just far enough so everything came into focus. The shelf on the wall looked like a wall in a pharmacy with lots of colorful bottles on it.

I awoke and knew I had been asleep, yet I was actively participating in the dream. I asked the vision to move. Not in words like we converse day-to-day with each other, but with my mind. The image responded; we communicated. Who was answering me and from where? I fell back asleep.

In front of me was a gold geometric figure multiplying itself times one hundred and all of them floating and moving in front of me in strict dance precision. I was watching a 3-D movie, only I didn't have any special glasses on to see it. The image of the geometric figure was imprinted in my mind.

Eleven days later, the same geometric figure was again shown to me.

One gold geometric shape floated in front of me, and I watched as the open spaces within it filled up with the number nine.

I woke up and drew a picture of the geometric figure in my journal and placed the number nine in each of the spaces. The next day, I entered all the earlier visions into my journal in chronological order, just like Beverly and Donna Marie had told me to do.

❈ ❈ ❈ ❈ ❈

On my first day of Reiki class, Donna Marie had a helper to assist her because the class was more significant in size than usual. The group consisted of a woman horse whisperer, two Catholic nuns, four physical therapists from a local hospital, my friend MaryAnn, and me.

At lunchtime, the helper scurried out to get to downtown Green Bay to see Joanne Koenig-Macko, a world-renowned spiritual painter from Naperville, Illinois, who was displaying her artwork, and then be back in time to help with the afternoon class.

When the helper returned, she brought with her three small lithograph pictures she had purchased from the artist. She was eager to share them with us, so she passed each image around the room for all to see.

The first picture passed around was beautiful. The second image handed to me immediately sent substantial, rolling chills through my body. Great music would give me chills, but artwork had never affected me before. The intensity of the rolling chills was stronger than I had ever experienced. It was a picture of a beautiful Native Indian maiden wearing a lovely shawl, and she had two inverted hearts that looked like they were weeping. When I passed it off to the next person, the rolling chills stopped. I held the third picture, and it too was nice, and I passed it on.

All the students arrived for our second day of class, and we met in Donna Marie's healing room. A massage table was off to the right side of the room with a pillow on it, and propped up in front of the pillow were the three pictures from the spiritual painter we had seen the day before. When my eyes scanned each photo, I again had substantial rolling chills go through my body when my eyes locked onto the Native Indian maiden. I knew I was being asked to pay attention.

I arrived home from my first weekend Reiki class, and I immediately went online and looked up Joanne

Koenig-Macko. I saw the painting of the Native Indian maiden called the *Angel of Mercy* on her website.

The painting had been inspired by a trip Joanne had taken to Sedona, Arizona, at a site called Bell Rock. Joanne had stood at the top of a mountain and felt the presence of many Native Americans who had walked the land many years ago, and she realized the atrocities they suffered at the hand of the white man as they were forced off the land they loved.

Joanne's website noted there was much meaning in this image. The painting is all about forgiveness and mercy and finding gratitude in all that we do. We must respect everyone no matter what skin color they may have. We are to work in oneness and unity. Joanne was led to an area in Illinois called Starved Rock, where again, many Native Americans perished long ago. She was deeply inspired to finish the painting.

I knew I wanted to have this picture, but the large lithograph cost $490, and it was more than I could afford at the time. I saved my money during the next year, and when it came time for my birthday, I called Joanne and told her how I had come to see this picture and how it affected me. We talked for about a half hour on the telephone and shared with each other some of our experiences.

When I got out my credit card to pay for the painting, I gave her the first four numbers on my card, 4444.

Joanne immediately stopped me and asked, "Do you know what those numbers mean?"

I said, "No, can you tell me?"

She said, "You are surrounded by angels, spirit guides, and ascended masters at all times."

The lump in my throat left me speechless.

Joanne said, "I wish I could spend a week with you."

I replied, "I can't give you a week, but I could do a weekend." Joanne invited me to come to her home in Naperville the next month.

I hung up the telephone, floating on air. I was giddy inside like a kid seeing a decorated Christmas tree with presents under it on Christmas morning. I never supposed I would meet this artist in person, much less be invited to her home.

The lithograph painting I had ordered arrived a few days later. I opened it up and noticed Joanne had included a brochure from her earlier 2002 Annual Lightworkers Conference, which featured the *Angel of Mercy* painting on the back cover of the pamphlet. I opened the booklet to read about the conference, and I saw the gold geometric figure that had appeared in my two earlier visions. It was called the *Gate of Light*, and it was a golden pendant with eight stones on it. One of the stones was tanzanite. The brochure explained, "The stone (tanzanite leaves an opening for energy to pass through) transforms negative energy to positive. The negative energy is attracted to the *Gate of Light*. The new stone makes way for releasing the converted energy."

I sat down to catch my breath when I saw it. I thought I had been hit from behind with a baseball bat. If the Divine wanted me to listen up, it had my full attention. Here was the first incident I could go back to in my journal and compare the geometric figure I had drawn to the photo in the brochure. I also revisited the reading from Donna Marie about the stone called tanzanite.

✳ ✳ ✳ ✳ ✳

Upon arrival at Joanne's home, she put the *Gate of Light* pendant in my hand as I stood in the foyer of her house.

I asked her, "Why did I see this in a dream?"

She replied, "Because you're supposed to have it." She also advised me, "It was made in Israel."

A room just to the left of her front door entrance was filled with many paintings resting on easels. They were all dimensional looking, and one was more beautiful than the other. I asked Joanne if I could go in and look at them. She took me into the room and told me every painting was an original.

She said, "I don't use paintbrushes. I only use things from nature, like twigs, leaves and my own fingers to create the paintings. The angels tell me what to paint, and I can't sell the originals. They all give off energy, and anyone passing by the house by car, on foot, or taking the commuter train, all benefit from the power of these paintings. The lithographs also give off energy."

The *Angel of Mercy* picture was speaking to me in volumes. My Native Indian background stirred when Joanne stated she used only things from nature to create her artwork. The inverted hearts symbolized Heaven and Earth and the bringing of these two worlds together with love, understanding, and forgiveness. A symbol of man was located in the hearts' center, and a waterfall was washing over him, representing the cleansing and forgiveness for what they had done.

The painting was speaking to me like a person holding a bullhorn at a demonstration and continually shouting out the message: *We are all one!*

Joanne mentioned, "The shawl the Native Indian maiden is wearing has the *Gate of Light* geometric figure in each square of her shawl. She is wearing a necklace with a charoite stone, only found near the Chara River in Eastern Siberia, Russia. It is a powerful crystal and especially important for healers, as it inspires one to be of service to others and to Spirit. Its energy reaches out to the one who has it to bring his or her gifts to the world so everyone can benefit.

"A mystical hawk is flying towards her as a spirit messenger. Chief Pontiac was seated on his horse at the edge of the woods in the background where Native Indian ancestral spirits were visible in the woods.

Joanne walked me across the hall to show me her *World Peace* painting hanging in her healing room. The angel told her to paint it, and when finished, she would speak before nations. She had painted the picture but did not initially understand the directive of speaking before nations.

During President Clinton's administration, she had received a call from Washington, D.C. asking if she could bring her *World Peace* painting to the United Nations. She would not send the original art piece alone, so she traveled with it. She was seated in the audience at the United Nations and was acknowledged for her artwork. Unbeknownst to her, they gave her a microphone and asked her to say a few words. Thus she spoke before Nations, and the angel's message was completed.

Joanne told me lithographs of her *World Peace* artwork had gone out all over the world and are owned by many ambassadors, world leaders, and peacemakers around the globe. To name a few, former President Rodrigo Carazo of

Costa Rica, Madeleine Albright, first woman Secretary of State of the United States, Mikhail Gorbachev, first President of the Soviet Union, and former President of Egypt, Hosni Mubarak, and many other world ambassadors. It had been sent to over thirty countries and the children of Medjugorje in Bosnia. It hangs in the U.S. Embassy in England, and other healing centers around the world.

The next day, Joanne told me, "Reiki is opening up a door for you." She asked, "Would you like me to do an Angel Therapy session with you? Of course I said yes. While I rested on her massage table, Joanne wrote down and drew five pages of things that had come through to her about me from the angels.

Divine Guidance is opening up your heart to love through direct experience with the celestial kingdom. Something significant and profoundly meaningful will further your reality of the Divine in your life. Over the next several days you'll be directly guided by the Universe. It could be through a poem, reading, vision, or you may encounter the spirit of a loved one or have a glimpse at the angels.

You also had lifetimes in Atlantis and Egypt as a priestess. You worked with energy healing crystals magnified by the sun in a rejuvenation temple. You had different rooms for various medicinal purposes and different crystals.

New knowledge is coming to the earth. The Pi sign becomes the doorway for you to walk through for the new knowledge. She drew the Pi sign with an angel floating in the center radiating light and energy out from it.

✖ ✖ ✖ ✖ ✖

Leaving her healing room, I saw a painting on the wall of an angel wearing a red cloak bending down and protecting a young woman sitting on a bench in front of a pond. It sent substantial rolling chills through me. Here we go again. *I was being hit by a cosmic 2x4 to pay attention.*

I asked Joanne, "Can you explain this painting to me?"

She replied, "It is the *Angel of Courage,* and she is bringing power, strength, and courage to the young woman crying in front of a meditation pond, complete with Japanese Koi fish, an iridescent blue dragonfly on one of the rocks, and an Irish fairy sleeping near the water."

I didn't know why, but I knew instantly the picture was for my sister. I purchased the *Angel of Courage* artwork and drove from Naperville, Illinois, to Portage, Wisconsin that evening to deliver it to her.

Upon my arrival in Portage, I showed it to my sister, and she wept. She told me, "Red is my favorite color, and I love the Koi fish from our travels in the world. The Irish fairy sleeping near the water reminds me of the Celtic side of our family background. The hibiscus flowers in the painting are my favorite."

I sensed the *Angel of Courage* was vital for her since she was suffering from three autoimmune diseases.

❦ ❦ ❦ ❦ ❦

Four days after visiting Joanne, I received the Divine Guidance event she told me about and humbly entered it into my journal.

I was sitting on a bright white stone bench on top of a hillside overlooking valleys of flowers for as far as the eye could see. The flowers were beautiful, and many of the colors were not of this earth. All the flowers were vibrating with a form of energy.

Sitting next to me was a tall male figure who looked like he was in his early thirties wearing a long white robe. Together we enjoyed the view of the flowers and the energy the colors were giving off. We communicated telepathically, and the presence told me he was my brother Michael. I instantly felt a depth of love and peace not available on the earth. Its power radiated through my heart and body with an explosion more massive than a thousand exploding suns, and I did not want the feeling to stop.

If this is what real love is and could be experienced in our world, I wanted to harness it and share it with mankind.

❧ ❧ ❧ ❧ ❧

I finished my Reiki classes in Green Bay and decided to take the Reiki Master Teacher course closer to home. I found my new teacher, Arline Rowden, near Madison, to help me accomplish my goal. I completed the course, and then signed up for Arline's six-month *Awakening Your Light Body* by Duane Parker and Sanaya Roman with their guides, DaBen and Orin. I had never meditated before, and I wanted some guidance on how to go about it.

The course was demanding and required 30 minutes every day of listening to tapes at home and a formal class with Arline every two weeks. I did this faithfully for four and a half months, and I did not experience anything. I persisted. I believe in the saying, "Don't stop just before the miracle happens." During the fifth month, I experienced pain in my head which brought tears to my eyes. The pressure in my head was so intense I didn't know what to do. When the tape ended, the pain stopped. That night, while lying in bed I heard a bold, resonating male voice say "106." I had no idea what the number meant.

At the next formal class with Arline, I told her what had happened regarding the pain in my head. She advised me, "The next time it happens, have the intention of the back of your head and neck to open up to allow for more energy flow and there would be less pressure." I also asked her if she knew what the number 106 meant.

She replied, "If you add the numbers together, they equal seven, which is a healing number."

During the remaining weeks of the fifth and sixth month, I started to experience visions during my meditation practices. I recorded them in my journal just as I was doing for the vivid dreams I had at night. I saw the following items during my meditation sessions.

- *A large white cross, similar to what is seen on an ambulance.*
- *A book floating in front of me with no title and nothing written on the pages.*
- *A sizeable five-pointed star floating in front of me and inside the five-pointed star was a cross radiating bright light outwardly.*

During the last meditation class with Arline, she played soft music and recited a guided meditation for the whole class.

As the meditation progressed, I saw the most beautiful gold crown floating above my head, and out of the center of it came beautiful bright colors shooting upward. When Arline brought us out of the meditation, my body was vibrating internally like an electric generator on high. I didn't say anything at first because I wasn't sure what was happening. I reached over to a classmate and touched her arm and asked if she could feel the vibration. She could not. I waited a little longer, and then I became concerned enough to tell Arline what I was feeling. The intensity of the vibration was like a high electrical current running through my body.

Arline asked me, "What are you afraid of?"

I replied, "I'm not scared of anything."

Arline stood up and told me to stand up in front of her, and she started to do Reiki on me. I could feel the heat radiating off of her hands as she held them just outside the outline of my body and never touched me. The vibration stopped.

❄ ❄ ❄ ❄ ❄

Beverly Kay had told me I was in tune with metaphysics and something active and new was on the horizon; I just couldn't see it yet.

Donna Marie Levy had told me I would understand quantum physics and the meaning of Pi (π), and I would be doing something that had not yet come to the earth.

Joanne Koenig-Macko had said the Pi sign (π) would become the doorway for me to walk through to find the new knowledge.

All three of them had told me I was a priest or priestess in a past lifetime, and all three knew my heart ached with sadness for my son.

When things come in threes, I always sit up and take notice. Now I had more exploring and research to do to understand where all of this was taking me.

🦋 🦋 🦋 🦋 🦋

"All the believers were one in heart and mind.
No one claimed that any of their possessions was their own,
but they shared everything they had."
—Acts 4:32 NIV

MY PHOTO ALBUM

My parents, William and Dolores
Collins, World War II

William, Dolores and Michael,
1952

My brother, Michael Collins, 1952

Dolores and William, 1993

The two far left windows were my Cell for six months.
Front left, Roman Centurion tree

Carolyn Awe, educator, and
daughter of Bob and Liz Awe and
youngest member of our
spiritual group

Friends Darcy Lutzow and Kurt
Pederson

Liz and Bob Awe at Dad's 90th birthday party

Friend Judy Broman in Arizona during shaman trip

Angel of Mercy, painted by Joanne Koenig-Macko

Angel of Courage, painted by Joanne Koenig-Macko

God's Country Crew, St. Germain, WI. Skipper Bob Reinen in front. Standing from L to R: Chaplain Kathy, Diane Reinen, and Liz Awe

William and Dolores Collins with neighbors Gert and Mike Lukens

Chakra necklace purchased
at art fair first year
in St. Germain, WI

Gate of Light necklace
seen in vision

Queen-sized heart quilt won at Curl for the Cure

Three rows on back of quilt with
hearts quilted on it

Chaplain Kathy
with heart quilt

CHAPTER SIX
ALTERNATIVES

"HELP—Hello Eternal Loving Presence"
—Michael Bernard Beckwith

My quest for more spiritual knowledge was turning my life around and making me look through my eyes, not with my eyes. I had become more aware of other healing traditions and practices, some ancient and some new age, all with a common thread of a Divine energy force. All understood the importance of our being connected as one with each other, with nature, with the infinite power of love from the heart binding everything.

❧ ❧ ❧ ❧ ❧

MaryAnn and I finished our Reiki Master Teacher classes and were eager to try our newfound energy relaxation/stress relief practice. We invited a mutual friend, Patty, to share the experience of doing Reiki on her. Patty had been diagnosed with systemic lupus, a chronic disease, that causes inflammation, tissue damage, and pain. She was open to trying anything that would give her body relief.

We invited her to our healing room where she was greeted with soft lighting and Thaddeus Angel music softly playing in the background. MaryAnn and I synchronized our newfound skills and did double Reiki on Patty for one hour. I started working on Patty's head while MaryAnn began to work on her feet, and we rotated clockwise around her body working over the seven chakra energy centers of her body. Our first patient had received twice the energy of an ordinary session with both of us working on her, and Patty went home grateful and very relaxed.

After Patty left, MaryAnn and I debriefed our technique. I was pleased with the timing of our synchronized movements around Patty's body, and I shared with MaryAnn, "I kept my eyes closed at each station I moved to."

MaryAnn remarked, "I kept my eyes open all the time, and I looked at you across the table and saw electrical streaks, like mini bolts of lightning, coming from all your fingers. It was beautiful!"

I never saw the light show coming from my fingers that MaryAnn told me about. It did not surprise me since I had been experiencing the feeling of a generator running through my body for other things, so why not this.

✖ ✖ ✖ ✖

After meeting the spiritual painter, Joanne Koenig-Macko, she asked me to attend her yearly Midwestern Lightworkers Conference in Naperville. My world was opening up to new awareness, so I registered for the conference. Her guest speaker was Dolores Cannon, who spoke about her Quantum Healing Hypnosis Therapy (QHHT). I was captivated by Dolores's presentation and the discussion about her published books filled with years of QHHT work. She was able to document conversations with a person's higher self from the past and the future, yet all coexisting in the *Now*.

While attending the conference, I met Patricia "Trish" Poole, a certified hypnotherapist and past life regressionist who had trained with Dolores Cannon. I took Trish's business card because she was from Green Bay, a city not far from Sun Prairie, just in case I'd like to try this alternative work. I put her card in my conference bag along with other conference information treasures obtained at the various presenter tables.

As I continued to stroll down the different aisles, I came upon a large group surrounding one of the booths. I couldn't see what they were doing, so I continued on. At that moment, I heard a familiar sound that permeated my entire body. It stopped me immediately. It sounded and felt familiar, yet I couldn't place it. I again heard the sound, and it reverberated through my body from head to toe. I stood back and waited for the crowd to disperse and then moved up to the table.

I spoke with a man named Gary, who was a friend of Joanne Koenig-Macko. Gary had written a book about Indigo children, and he was representing a young man at the conference said to be an Indigo child who created a gift to share at the conference. The young man produced a bright silver half-moon metal object and attached it to a beautifully stained wood platform. When it was struck with a soft mallet, it created the sound and vibration I had heard and felt. I purchased it. It would become my most treasured find at the conference.

After returning home, I started to use the metal object during my Reiki sessions to surround my patients with the vibration it gave off and to also continue to feel the vibration myself. It was as if every atom in my body was being called to attention when I experienced the reverberation of the sound.

❀ ❀ ❀ ❀ ❀

Seven months later, after reading all of the books I had purchased from Dolores Cannon at the Lightworker Conference, I reached out to Trish Poole for a past life regression. I approached this session with my usual "Doubting Thomas" skeptical attitude on high alert. I couldn't believe someone would be able to put me in a state of mind to get me to go back into a past life and see significant events during that life, and even experience my death if I so wished. My need to test and experiment with new modalities was taking me down a new highway, and it was as though I was just getting my driver's license.

I arrived at Trish's business address, and she had me remove my shoes and keep my socks on. I reclined on her massage table, and she stated she would be tape-recording the results of my past life regression. Trish explained to me that during the regression, she would be helping me move through the key events that make up the life I would be coming into. She stated when we were ready she would count down from (3) to (1) and at (1), I would be at the next relevant event where there is helpful information we'd like to find so we can know more about this lifetime.

I would then be asked to plant my feet firmly on the surface and tell Trish what I noticed. Trish noted most often the events take people up to and through their death and to the light for a life review or message from their Council.

Trish explained to me, "The body is like the clothing that an actor or actress wears, and at the end of the scene, they take off the clothing and carry on. That is how the soul is. The soul is the actor or actress, and the body is the clothing." Trish noted I would be able to visit the moment of my passing and find out what happened so that we could process the information. She also stated I would be able to watch my death as if it were happening to someone else or however I wanted to experience it. Trish said I would also experience my going into the light for a life review, such as: *What is it that you did well? What is the connection between that lifetime and this one? Can we do some healing with it?*

Trish stated, "I will have you stay in the light for any kind of healing or a message from your Council. If you don't remember your death or a specific message from your Council, it may be downloaded, and it will be put off until later when it is relevant or until you need to know."

Trish started the tape recorder...

Trish started speaking softly and the next thing I remember she was asking me to look down and plant my feet on the surface and she invited me to tell her what I saw.

I replied, "My feet are bare. I'm running through tall wispy grass along a river bank on a bright sunny day.

Trish asked, "How old are you?"

I responded, "I'm five years old."

Trish asked, "Can you describe yourself?"

I told her, "I have dark skin, and I'm naked with long, shiny black hair. I can see many beautiful blue butterflies rising up from the edge of the river bank from the rocks they were sitting on, and surrounding me with their playful beauty. As they are flying around me their bright metallic blue top and dull brown bottom colors flash. They look like they are appearing and disappearing around me in a blink of an eye. I'm connecting with them."

I heard Trish say, "If we are ready to move on, I will count down from (3) to (1), and you will arrive at your next relevant event." I heard her soft voice say, "Three, two, one. Look down at your feet and plant them firmly on the surface and tell me what you see."

I replied, "My feet are covered in animal hide.

After a brief pause, Trish asked, "Tell me what you see."

I replied, "I'm observing the older women in the village at work."

Trish asked, "How old are you?"

I told her, "I'm ten years old."

Trish asked, "What are the older women doing?"

I responded, "They are stripping the carcass of an animal. Everyone has a particular job. Nothing is going to waste. I'm being shown how it is done. I have to learn so I will be able to help them. I don't like what I'm seeing, hearing or smelling. I don't like this."

I heard Trish say, "If we are ready to move on I will count down from (3) to (1), and you will arrive at your next relevant event." I heard her soft voice say, "Three, two, one. Look down at your feet and plant them firmly on the surface and tell me what you see."

I replied, "My feet are still covered with animal hide, and the hide looks worn.

Trish asked, "How old are you?"

I told her, "I'm 15 years old. I'm walking with my tribe. We are all moving to a new location. I'm walking next to a woman who is ill and too weak to walk. I want to stay at her side. The woman is slowly being pulled behind a horse, and we are lagging behind the overall tribe."

Trish asked, "Who is the woman you are walking next to?" I replied, "It is my mother."

I heard Trish say, "If we are ready to move on I will count down from (3) to (1), and you will arrive at your next relevant event." I heard her soft voice say, "Three, two, one. Look down at your feet and plant them firmly on the surface and tell me what you see."

I told her, "I'm wearing different shoes. They are confining."

Trish asked, "How old are you?"

I said, "I'm 18 years old. I'm helping a family in their dry goods store. I'm sweeping the floor. They want me to stay out of sight when people come into their store. I feel invisible. I'm alone, and no longer with my birth family. Being alone and different from others is overwhelming."

I heard Trish say, "If we are ready to move on I will count down from (3) to (1), and you will arrive at your moment of death." I heard her soft voice say, "Three, two, one. Look down at your feet and plant them firmly on the surface and tell me what you see."

I replied, "I'm in a chamber yet there are no walls. There are brilliant beams of light being emitted from all around. I'm experiencing a tremendous feeling of calm and peace. I'm standing in front of a long, beautiful, white stone table. There are many beings around the table, and each one is emitting its own bright light. I've seen these beings before, and I'm comfortable in their presence. They're telling me they never left me when I thought I was alone. They are biblical looking, and some are Native Indian.

Trish then brought me out of the regression.

Trish apologized that the recording of my regression didn't work and I, needless to say, was disappointed that I didn't have a tape to refer to.

The experience I had during this past life regression was one of being in two places at one time. Seeing the past and hearing Trish speak to me in the present. Everything was happening simultaneously. The same feeling I had with Barb Krull during my hot-stone massage a few years earlier when I went out into the cosmos.

Describing the walk alongside my mother as an Indian girl reminded me of my mom sitting next to my bed when I was recouping from cancer in this current lifetime.

Seeing the bright metallic-blue butterflies reminded me of my current childhood days collecting butterflies and any insects I could find to study them. I spent whatever free time I had as a child out in nature. It lifted my spirits and gave me a place to feel whole. It was my escape from feeling unseen and not valued while growing up. Yet I never saw or caught a blue-metallic butterfly like I had seen in the session. *They were unusual and exquisite.*

Seeing the faces of the men around the bright white Council table was another answer to a vision I recorded in my journal about the human faces swiftly coming toward me. All my life, I have been terrible at remembering people's names, but I never forget a face. This time was no different. We had all met before this session with Trish.

Donna Marie referred to these beings as my Heavenly Council. I'm trying hard to wrap my mind around all of this, yet I was being shown I'm in excellent company and I'm never alone, even though I can't always see them.

Note to Reader:

In researching my book, I reconnected with Trish Poole to get the exact wording that she uses in her past life regressions. What I have written about this event is as factual as I can make it from her side, and I have shared exactly the things that were seared into my mind and heart of what I experienced and remembered. Apparently, I did not recognize my death or experience my life review that I could remember. Trish explained to me, my past death or any message information from my life review may have been downloaded and will be revealed when it is relevant.

During my revisit with Trish, she stated, "Spirit works in strange ways. There may have been a good reason why the recording did not work that day."

I told Trish, "I feel there is a strong reason I reconnected with you after all these years. Time will tell."

❦ ❦ ❦ ❦ ❦

Shamanism, being the oldest recorded healing tradition in the world, and a part of my Native Indian background from past generations, would be my next point of exploration. I started looking on the Internet for information on shamans and found a shamanic master healer and spiritual teacher in Sedona. I took a deep breath and called him to arrange a private meeting. A trip to meet a shaman in Sedona was the polar opposite of my regular, everyday life. I wanted to walk through all doorways available to me to the ancient teachings of healing and connecting with nature and hopefully get more answers to what was happening to me.

❦ ❦ ❦ ❦ ❦

My friend Judy Broman was willing to accompany me on this trip, knowing I would have to leave her alone for a few days while I worked with the shaman. Judy and I had met at work and became good friends about the same time I met Darcy. All three of us became BFFs.

We would all go to lunch every Wednesday, and I began to share with them more of my visions and messages. Darcy was aware of our initial summer weekend event, but as I started to share more with both of them of what was happening to me, they reacted a bit uncertainly, and then I saw them make eye contact and both had smirks on their faces. As I continued to share with them, in time they both agreed, "You just can't make this stuff up." As time went on, they would ask me at each weekly lunch, "What's new since we last met?"

🐦 🐦 🐦 🐦 🐦

Judy and I arrived at Phoenix International Airport, rented a car and headed out on our two-hour drive to Sedona on Interstate 17. The Phoenix landscape was drab and flat with intermittent sightings of various sized cactus plants along the roadway. The lack of color in my overall view left me wondering if I was in the wrong place. I loved to see color and Phoenix just wasn't stepping up to the plate to meet my expectations.

As we climbed higher into the winding hillsides outside of Phoenix and skirted along the outer edge of the Tonto National Forest, more green started to appear from the scrawny pine trees filling the horizon. The pine trees were a disappointment compared to the tall, billowing and healthy pine trees of lush northern Wisconsin, but it was a vast improvement from Phoenix. I was missing the dominant color of green from back home.

As we drove up and over a crest of the highway, both of us were transported into another world of immeasurable splendor. As far as we both could see was a sea of red rock monoliths jutting out of the green foliage skirts surrounding their bases. The canyon we drove into was lush with intense red color. It looked like someone had taken a knife and cut a line across the landscape. One side was dull and drab, and the other was bright and colorful. Our dispositions changed, and we both agreed this was more like it. We were ready to begin our vacation quest.

As we entered the outer edge of Sedona, we stopped at a four-way intersection. While waiting for the traffic light to change, a red-tailed hawk swooped down and over the top of our rental car at windshield level. It startled Judy, but I was used to this happening and sensed it to be an unequivocal message, *"Welcome to Sedona. We've been waiting for you."*

The trees along the Oak Creek River, running through Sedona and behind our hotel, did not yet have their leaves. During the night, the weather turned unusually warm for March, and by morning, all the trees along the river bank of the Oak Creek had blossomed out. As Judy and I looked out our hotel patio windows the following day, it looked like an artist had come through with a paintbrush and palette, and with delicate strokes filled in all the trees with color. Our stark winter view had turned into a lush springtime painting in less than 24-hours. Store owners and tourists were all talking about it. Many were bothered with severe allergy issues because it came so fast. The locals referred to it as a "super blast."

I met the shaman mid-morning at his office, just a few blocks from our hotel. I thought I would be going out into the hills and the Sedona red rocks to work with him in nature, but instead, the shaman told me our first day of work would be in his office.

"Please sit down and be comfortable," he directed.

As I sat down across from him, I watched as he ignited a sage smudge and waved it around to perform the ancient cleansing ritual used by Native American and shamanic cultures to bless the space we were in and remove all negative energy.

The shaman then asked, "Tell me why you came to see me."

I replied, "I'm hoping I can get answers to why I'm receiving visions and messages and find out what it all means."

There was a momentary silence in the room. The shaman replied, "I don't think so. I believe you came to see me about your son."

I was speechless when he mentioned my son because I had not mentioned him at all. I was traumatized by his remark and thought to myself, "*I didn't come halfway across the country to talk about my son who I had not heard from for five years.*" In defiance, I immediately crossed my legs and crossed my arms in front of my body. The shaman was going into territory I wasn't prepared to discuss, and I had been blocking it out and avoiding the pain it caused in my heart for the last number of years.

The shaman looked directly at me and replied, "You just spoke volumes to me when you crossed your arms and legs. Do you want to tell me about it?"

I replied, "There isn't much I can say to you. My son decided to cut himself off from our family without telling us why. Not just from me, but also from his grandfather and grandmother, my sister and her family and my brother."

I sensed a calmness come over the room. The pain in my heart was ready to release, and I started to reveal my pain story to a shamanic healer.

Our family had received an invite to my son's second child's christening. Before the service started, I was alone with my son in the back of the church, and asked, "Will your father be coming today?"

He replied emphatically, "I don't want him here." My son then walked away from me.

Even though his father and I were divorced, the christening was a significant event in his newborn daughter's life, and I wondered why he would not invite his father to be a part of the church celebration with him. His father had not been asked to their first child's christening either.

I sat in the back of the church with my grandson and his other grandmother to keep him busy and entertained during the service, so his mom and dad could rest easy during the christening service of his new baby sister.

I asked the other grandmother if she knew a friend of my son who was sitting a few rows ahead of us and had attended high school with her daughter and my son. She didn't know him.

I told her, "My son always told me when he gets married he wanted his friend Eddie to be his best man."

The other grandmother turned to me and in a repellant voice like a mother protecting her cubs from danger said, "They are married, and they've been married for some time."

I asked in a dazed and questioning tone, "When did they get married?"

She replied, "They were married before their son was born, but you didn't hear it from me."

My heart sank with humiliated, crushing pain. Not just for my own disappointment in my son's not telling me, but I thought more about my daughter-in-law and how she must have felt that he didn't believe it was essential to convey to his family he married her. I know I would have been upset had I been in my daughter-in-law's shoes. All of my family loved her from the first time we met her. We were all left clueless as to why my son cut himself off from us.

Before any of this had happened, each summer, the three of them would come to visit us for a weekend. When I was alone with my son, I would ask him, "When are we going to hear wedding bells for you and our grandson's mom?"

He always responded, "I want to finish college first."

This breaking news announcement from my daughter-in-law's mother made me wonder why my son would want our family to think he wasn't married for this entire time.

In my numb state of mind, my purse dropped to the floor with a massive bang. I bent down to pick it up and gather all the items that had fallen out of it. I took my time retrieving the scattered pieces so I could compose myself and wipe the tears welling up in my eyes. The shock of this news was staggering. I always thought births, marriages, and deaths to be significant milestones for individuals and their families to witness whenever possible or to be made aware of.

When I sat back up on the church bench, I asked my daughter-in-law's mother, "Can you tell me the wedding date so I can acknowledge their marriage in the future?"

She replied, "I can't remember the month and day at this time."

My daughter-in-law came from a large family, and I'm sure I too would have to refer to a record book for all the specific milestone dates of her mother's children and grandchildren, so I never received the information I requested.

I had offered to drive my parents from Sun Prairie to Oshkosh, Wisconsin to the christening event. With this unexpected announcement, I wished I had traveled by myself, so I could have quietly walked out of the church and left. No one would have been the wiser as to where I had gone and why. The hurt I was feeling was immeasurable. I took slow, deep breaths to keep myself composed while my daughter-in-law's mother and I sat silently in the pew, with our grandson between us, for the rest of the christening service.

After the christening ceremony, everyone was invited to my son and daughter-in-law's apartment. It was the first time my family and I were able to meet all of my daughter-in-law's family. I didn't let on to anyone in my family about what happened in church because I didn't want to cause any dilemmas for my daughter-in-law's mother, but I honestly wished I had been able to leave before the church service ended.

My daughter-in-law's mother never came out of the kitchen to join the other guests in the living room where my family was mingling with my daughter-in-law's siblings and their spouses. I sensed she had told my daughter-in-law what happened and probably wondered if I would say anything about the secret she revealed to me in front of the families. I had no ill feelings towards her, and was very grateful she told me. At least someone had the decency to bring me up to speed on the wedding event.

When Mom, Dad, and I left their apartment to begin our return drive home, I asked, "Do either of you know about your grandson being married?" They both were shocked into silence at what I had asked, and I could see in the rearview mirror of the car the look of surprise on both of their faces. It was a hushed ride back to Sun Prairie.

A week later, a letter arrived from my son. Both Mom and Dad were waiting to hear what the message had to reveal and I shared it with them. He wrote he owed us all an apology, and he would come and talk to all of us, including my sister. We never heard from him, and he never came.

A few years later, our daughter-in-law reached out and asked if she could come in the summer with the grandchildren to visit for a weekend. We were ecstatic and admired her immensely for it since my son refused to come.

She brought the children every August for a weekend visit, and they would get together with my sister's children for cousin bonding. We were all delighted they had a chance to get to know our side of the family as brief as our time was with them.

After the second year visit, I asked my daughter-in-law, "Why didn't my son tell me you two were married?"

Her response was, "He's chicken." I felt the response was unusual and she didn't elaborate any further. I wondered what my son was afraid of. My entire family did not understand *why he would feel this way since he was of age to make his own decisions.*

I wished my daughter-in-law could have told us they were married as well, but I completely understood it was her husband's responsibility to tell his family about the woman he loved and would be the mother of his children.

I kept the letter my son wrote and planned to give the message to my daughter-in-law so we could discuss it, but since she didn't want to elaborate on why this all happened, I decided I didn't want to pursue it any further with her. I would remain in the dark as to why my son did not want to share the news of his marriage and wanted me and my family to think he wasn't married at all.

I also told my family I could no longer discuss this situation because it was too painful for me. I had closed my heart and resigned myself to never seeing my son again.

I finished telling the shaman what I knew. In between a river of tears and wiping my sore nose with every tissue from a full box of Kleenex, I stated matter of factly, "I have no answer as to why this all happened the way it did, and neither do my parents or my sister's family. If you can enlighten me, I'd appreciate it. I learned to bury this pain for so long, and I certainly didn't expect to travel from Wisconsin to Arizona and share it with you today."

The shaman responded gently, "You need to reach out to your son."

I asked reluctantly, "Why? He apparently doesn't want my family or me in his life."

The shaman continued to speak gently, "You need to reach out to him so you can move forward on your journey.

If he doesn't accept your gesture, the situation will be totally on him only."

The shaman got up from his chair and went over to a bookshelf and pulled out a book titled *Your Best Life Now* by Joel Osteen, then handed it to me. He stated, "It's my personal book, but I want you to read it and keep it." We ended our first session with the understanding we would meet the next day to work outside in nature.

I returned to the hotel where Judy was patiently waiting for me so we could do a few tourist things before the day was over. Upon entering our hotel room, I saw Judy's surprised facial expression, and she remarked, "What happened to you? Your eyes are swollen."

I responded, "The session was very intense and emotional. It was not at all what I had expected." I put a cold cloth compress on my eyes and rested for a while. I did not elaborate any further with Judy about my session.

I had never shared my heartache with any of my friends about my son. Not mentioning his name kept the pain buried in my heart. Sharing my discomfort with the shaman let me release it. I was once told tears are a form of healing. If so, I must be healed because I shed enough to fill a ten-gallon water bucket.

❦ ❦ ❦ ❦ ❦

The next morning, the shaman and I met at his office, and he drove me to the Red Rocks, where we walked the spiritual path waiting for me. As we walked, the shaman led the way while chanting and slowly and methodically beating a handheld drum made of wood and deerskin with a totem of a panther on it.

The vista of the Red Rocks from our vantage point was spectacular. As we progressed along the chosen path, the shaman stopped and asked me to step just off the foot-path and stand in the middle of a split tree trunk that had grown over nine feet high on each side. Keeping my body upright within the opening was like being on a balance beam fighting to hold my space. While standing in the opening of the tree, I had a flashback to my childhood when I stealthily climbed every possible tree within a two-block radius of my home. The flashback was a picturesque, golden gift of memory from the ancient spirits to show me my early, natural, playful connection to Mother Earth. The shaman asked me to exit the tree, and we strolled further along the spiritual path as he continued to chant and methodically beat his drum.

Our next stop along the way was a natural electro-magnetic field called a vortex. At the shaman's direction, I stepped off the path and into the center of the vortex.

The shaman returned to the pathway, and I quietly waited where he asked me to stand. A swirling wind, embedded with fine particles of Mother Earth's dust, started to eddy around my shoes and ankles as it ascended upward along the outline of my body to above my head. As the energy embraced me, I heard the rhythmical beat of a heart keeping time with the pulse of the vortex. When the sound of the heartbeat stopped, I heard the shaman ask, "Step out of the vortex and return to the footpath." I was thunderstruck.

We moved further along the sacred path as the shaman continued to chant and beat his sacred drum. At our final destination, the shaman pointed and said, "Step off the path and stand in front of the pine tree." There was a six-foot pine tree growing just a few feet off of the pathway. The shaman directed, "Wrap your arms around the pine tree, close your eyes, and give it a bear hug."

I thought his request was one of humor and I asked, "Are you serious?"

He responded, "The pine tree has something to share with you." I trusted his wisdom and did what he asked, but I was glad no one I knew was there to see me cuddling a prickly pine tree.

The message from the pine tree was a pale yellow circle of energy dancing in front of me. I now had a third color in my healing toolbox, along with the previously seen green and purple colors on my awakening quest. The shaman asked me to return to the sacred path.

As I approached him, he had a smile on his face and said, "You will share your gift."

The magnificent Red Rocks of Sedona invited me into their mystical and guarded ways of the ancients, and I was grateful and humbled by their warm and welcoming hospitality.

ЖЖЖЖЖ

I finished reading the book the shaman had given me before I returned home. The book discussed the importance of releasing fear and extending forgiveness to those who hurt us. We need to move on even though we don't have any answers as to why, and trust and let God handle it. It was teaching the importance of extending forgiveness to those who hurt us and to ourselves for holding the negative thoughts so we can open up to the beauty of compassion for others and self-compassion for ourselves. It also reminded me the Divine is always giving us tests, and when we pass them, we advance forward because adversity often pushes us into our divine destiny.

Judy and I finished out our week enjoying the sights, shops, and restaurants of Sedona and a tour and view of the Grand Canyon. I enjoyed picking out gifts to take back home for the family, including my two grandchildren.

Upon my return home, I checked my *Chakra Clearing* book to see what the pale yellow color meant. The reference stated, "Emerging psychic and spiritual awareness; optimism and hopefulness; positive excitement about new ideas."

🦋 🦋 🦋 🦋 🦋

Every May over Memorial Day weekend, I make a two-hour pilgrimage to Michael's grave site in Lake Church, Wisconsin. Every year, I wash and clean his gravestone and put ornamental flowers on his grave to honor his life. This year I decided I would make a side trip afterward to see my son who lived 15 minutes away. I had mixed emotions about doing it, but I remembered what the shaman told me about not being able to move forward on my journey if I didn't.

I brought along the Sedona gifts for my grandchildren, and hoped my son would be home and receptive to my unannounced visit. Normally, I would have called in advance, but I didn't think my son would make himself available if he knew I was coming. I wasn't even sure anyone would be home, but I made an effort to try. I would not be back in this area for another year.

I knocked on the front door and my grandson opened the door. I said, "Good morning. Is your dad home?" My grandson opened the door wide to let me in, and I stayed in the front foyer, just inside the front door. My grandson disappeared around the corner to get his dad and then came back out and jumped up on the living room couch to continue watching his interrupted Saturday morning cartoons.

My son came from around the corner and curtly remarked, "What are you doing here?"

I responded, "I came to see you." I then turned to my grandson and said, "We are all looking forward to your visit in August. Your cousins are looking forward to getting together with you and your sister." My grandson responded with an affirming nod of his head and a big smile.

I turned back to my son, and he replied in a stern and direct tone, "I think you should leave." I turned around to open the inside front door, and my son came up on my right side, and helped to push the outside metal door open and held it as I passed through. He remarked quietly as he leaned over my right shoulder and into my right ear, "It would have been nice if you would have called first."

I inquired, "Would it have made any difference?"

He responded offhandedly, "Maybe."

I answered back, "I don't think so." I left the property without getting to give my grandchildren their gifts from Sedona. As I drove back to Sun Prairie, I realized that not giving them their gifts was my biggest disappointment of the day.

❌ ❌ ❌ ❌ ❌

The month of August came, and our family eagerly awaited the arrival of our daughter-in-law and the grandchildren for their yearly weekend visit. When they arrived, I asked the grandchildren to come into my bedroom, because I had a surprise for them. We all went into the bedroom. My grandson jumped up on my bed, and my granddaughter followed suit. I brought out their gifts from Sedona, and before I handed them to them, I told them, "I wanted to give you these gifts when I came to your house in May, but I didn't have a chance."

My grandson immediately interjected, "Grandma, what my dad did to you was wrong."

What my grandson said let me know he was aware of his father's actions and he understood. It was all I needed to know to move forward. My grandson's innocent and heartfelt remark took whatever lingering sadness that remained in my heart away forever. My grandson was a blessing from the Divine from the day he was born. Little did I know he would become the ray of love and light that helped me to move forward on my journey with a new open, and awakened heart.

❦❦❦❦❦

I met Kathleen Raven Wildwood, founder and director of The Wildwood Institute in Madison at a wellness fair. Her credentials stated she had studied and practiced in scientific, shamanic and Western herbal and intuitive traditions for over 20 years. She also taught workshops in Madison at Meriter Hospital, UW Medical School, and Edgewood College. Kathleen had been in private practice and teaching herbalism since 1996.

I signed up for one of her weekend workshops in my quest for alternative healing methods. While attending, I met other women interested in her teachings as well. When lunchtime came around on the first day, we were all on our own for an hour. A number of us went to a local café to grab a bite to eat and get to know each other.

One of the ladies talked about her recent trip to Sedona, and the new color therapy called Aura-Soma. I mentioned I had just returned from working with a shaman in Sedona and had not heard of it.

The woman stated, "It was all over Sedona. I can't believe you didn't see anything about it."

I commented, "I didn't get to check out any alternative healing places while I was there." The woman promised to bring me a copy of the Aura-Soma book she purchased while in Sedona to our next day's class so I could see it.

The next day at lunch, as promised, the lady handed me the *Aura-Soma Sourcebook—Color Therapy for the Soul* by Mike Booth with Carol McKnight. I was speechless when I saw it. The cover of the book had colored bottles on it just like I had seen in my previous vision of colored bottles on a shelf. I was able to again confirm that another image in my journal was what I was now looking at.

The book explained the bottles consisted of bringing together the oily and watery parts of plants, ground-up gems and crystals, and mineral energies acting as receivers and transmitters, and natural colorings that gave off vibrations and connected with our soul. It was a form of self-discovery through color. Each bottle had two colors. The upper fraction of the glass container represented the conscious mind, and the lower portion served the unconscious. The book also pointed out this was the same correlation noted by well-known psychiatrist, Carl Gustav Jung, and how he looked at a mandala with his patients.

Seeing the Aura-Soma colored bottles reminded me of our earlier family trips to Sun Prairie to visit my sister. My sister always wanted Mom and me to come and visit on Saturday so she could go to the quilt shop to purchase material and supplies for her quilt projects. I was not always thrilled with the idea of driving from Port Washington to Sun Prairie and spending most of our day at the quilt shop. I never expressed my discontent, but I would much rather have visited with my sister than walk around the quilt shop for hours.

Often, I would enter the quilt shop in a somewhat dark mood because of my discontent. As my sister did her shopping, I would walk around the aisles of fabric consisting of many varieties of hues from the color spectrum. The shop was organized according to the rays of the rainbow. I moved around the store from one shade of color to another and often times touched the colored fabric. By the time we all got back in the car to return to my sister's house, I was uplifted and happy.

It took a few more reluctant visits to the quilt store to realize what was happening to me. The colors were speaking to me and lifting my spirit. Who would have guessed it!

Is this what Michael was showing me in my vision when we sat together and watched the colored flowers vibrating in the valley for as far as the eye could see? I still needed those few missing pieces of the puzzle.

✺ ✺ ✺ ✺ ✺

"O Lord my God, I cried to you for help, and you healed me."
—Psalm 30:2 NIV

CHAPTER SEVEN

HEARTS, BUTTERFLIES, AND NUMBERS

"You must find the place inside yourself
where nothing is impossible."
—Deepak Chopra

After seeing the green and purple hearts floating in front of me, I became extremely aware of hearts being shown to me in various fashions. People started sending me cards with hearts on them. If they had before this, I just wasn't sensitive to noticing them. I had purchased a black purse and realized when I got it home, the embossed portion of the bag was all hearts. I was given a necklace from a friend returning from the Philippines, and it had a heart on it. While looking at the *Angel of Mercy* painting, I found a new heart within the picture that I hadn't seen when I initially received it.

When I started doing more Reiki, I asked my sister if she would make me a cover-up quilt for the people I worked on. When I got it, it was made of multicolored purples, greens, and pinks, and in each square of the quilt, she quilted a heart.

The hearts just kept on coming…

✼ ✼ ✼ ✼ ✼

Fall in Wisconsin is my favorite season, especially when the tree colors are changing and the air is so crisp it brings pink to my cheeks. Mom and I decided to take a ride on a beautiful Saturday morning from Sun Prairie to Portage to take in the first Pink Ribbon Angel Curling Bonspiel at the local curling club. This not-for-profit fund raising event was put together to help breast cancer patients in Columbia County with their out-of-pocket expenses when dealing with this devastating disease. The purpose of this labor of love was something very near and dear to my own heart, having experienced cancer and the dread of figuring out how to rob from Peter to pay Paul while I couldn't work.

Too many families are overwhelmed when they find out their insurance doesn't cover all the expenses of their treatments. Families of the cancer patients are given another blow to the midsection when their daily income is affected, and they can't pay their everyday bills. This not-for-profit organization of volunteers was just getting off the ground. Their mission of love was to help make those payments that insurance didn't cover and help pay for other out-of-pocket expenses life threw at the victims experiencing the disease. The bottom line was to make the patients as worry-free as possible so they could concentrate on getting themselves well without additional fearful thoughts of financial stress.

Pink Ribbon Angels was started by my sister and four other local women in the Portage community. They were also able to work with a hospital in the county to help pay for yearly mammograms of patients who did not have insurance coverage.

Mom and I were looking forward to this jam-packed, all-day experience. It included a substantial silent auction of items the community donated, time to watch the curling teams that came from all over the state to compete, and enjoy our lunch and dinner, which were included in our fee to attend this much-needed event.

Upon arrival, raffle tickets were sold to promote a queen-sized quilt handmade by the Pink Ribbon Angels. It was to be given away as the grand prize after the evening dinner. Mom and I each bought a raffle ticket to help support the cause.

As we walked further into the curling club, we perused the silent auction tables to see what we would be interested in bidding on. When we finished signing our pocketbooks away on the auction items we wanted to bid on, I turned to look back through the curling club to see how many people had come in. The room was filled with a sea of pink hats, jackets, T-shirts, and festive table decorations in honor of October's Breast Cancer Awareness month. The energy and excitement in the curling club were building. Everyone was there to help the cause and enjoy the camaraderie of the game of curling.

I looked up and saw the grand prize quilt hanging on the far wall in its full glorious presentation. The quilt had a big heart that seemed to float in the middle of a light golden-tan background fabric. The heart had purple fabric at the top, and green material at the bottom. The top and bottom of the heart were connected on the sides with a bronzy gold/green fall-colored fabric. Purple appliqued flowers with light gold centers with green stems and leaves extended outwardly and floated freely in the upper left and lower right corners of the quilt. The four outer borders of the quilt were green, purple, green, and again the bronzy/green fall colors completed the outside perimeter of the quilt.

My immediate thought was, *"What a beautiful labor of love."* At that moment, I began to see the three inner borders of green, purple, and green start to shimmer. It looked like tiny stars twinkling back at me around all four sides of the quilt. I watched with amazement and then asked Mom, who was standing next to me, "Mom, can you see the borders of the quilt shimmering?"

She replied, "No, I don't see anything."

I continued to watch the beautiful light show obviously being shown only to me. I could also hear the sound of a beating heart. When both stopped, I had a knowing come over me, and I walked up to the front of the room where the Pink Ribbon Angels were selling the raffle tickets. My sister walked up alongside me, and I told her, "You can sell all the raffle tickets you want today, but I'm going to win the grand prize quilt."

She looked at me stupefied and blew me off with her quick response, "Just buy more raffle tickets and take your chances like everybody else." She then walked away to handle other pressing matters for the event.

The evening dinner was well attended. There wasn't an empty seat in the curling club and Mom and I were seated in the middle of the room. The final event of the evening was about to take place. Everyone watched as a local doctor was asked to give the barrel of raffle tickets a good spin. When the barrel became stationary, my sister asked the doctor, "Please pull out the winning raffle ticket and hand it to me."

As the ticket was being pulled from the barrel, I stood up and stood behind my chair facing towards the front of the room. I watched as the doctor handed the ticket to my sister to read off the winning name. My sister's face turned into a look of complete disbelief as she looked at the name on the ticket. I watched her scan the room to find me. When she saw me standing in the middle of the room, she then announced my name. When I went up to the front to receive the grand prize, she asked in total disbelief, "How did you know?" I just smiled.

When I arrived home that evening, I hurriedly took the quilt to my bedroom to see if it would fit my bed correctly. As I unfolded the quilt, I noticed the stitching on the back of the quilt. To my amazement, the three rows of the border I had seen shimmering on the front of the quilt, had hearts quilted on the back of them around the entire four sides of the quilt. I picked up the quilt and embraced it tightly to my chest as tears ran down my face while I experienced rolling chills through my body. I pulled out my journal and wrote down an affirmation of how I wanted a healing center that would draw the best in the world to come to it to help others. I also wanted the heart quilt to be hanging up high in a place of honor for all to see when they entered the healing center. It would be a beacon of hope to all who walked through its doors.

After I wrote it down, I realized, *I don't have the money to make this kind of wish happen,* yet I was compelled to write it down on paper.

✖ ✖ ✖ ✖ ✖

As I contemplated the beauty of the quilt and my reaction to it, I recalled my Reiki training. Learning Reiki had taught me the colors of the seven energy centers in our body. The fourth heart chakra energy center was electric green and represented love, balance, and compassion. The hue for the seventh crown chakra energy center was electric purple, and it expressed spiritual connection, understanding, knowing, bliss, and oneness. Whenever both of these color centers were shown to me, I always heard the beating sound of a heart. I understood the Divine was connected within all of us through our hearts and brains. There was a knowing that we are never alone because the Divine spark resides inside all our hearts. When we open the door to our heart and let our trust in the Divine pour forth, no request is too small or too large. The Divine will lead and direct.

I realized what was in one's heart had to be genuinely felt, or it meant nothing. If you have a dream in your heart and no deep-down feeling about it, it isn't going to happen. It's like the Pharaoh of Egypt having all the straw he needed and no mud to create his bricks. It's the Universal Law of manifestation. The dream and the feeling must become one.

I became more intuitively aware of others' needs and each day, I also knew my daily job in the business world was not where I was supposed to be, yet I attentively watched and listened for guidance to show me where I was to go. The loving messages and nudges from the Divine I had been receiving, and the importance of the theme of the heart, were being shown to me in very creative ways.

ₓ ₓ ₓ ₓ ₓ

I began to seek out seminars and was drawn to well-known spiritual authors and presenters. John Holland, and his ability to connect with spirit on the other side. Marianne Williamson, and her understanding of love and peace for the world. Sonja Choquette, and her teachings of energy and spirit of the heart. Deepak Chopra, and his interest in alternative medicine, meditation, and in ancient healings and Dr. Brian Weiss, with his cures through past life regressions.

❈ ❈ ❈ ❈ ❈

Just before the Christmas holiday, my good friend Liz handed me a book titled *Proof of Heaven* by Eben Alexander, M.D. about his near-death experience (NDE). She thought I would be interested in reading it. When she handed it to me, I immediately began to weep. On the cover of the book was a Blue Morpho butterfly. It was the first time I had seen this beautiful butterfly since I had my past life regression. I was taken aback by my tearful reaction to seeing it.

I began to research the Blue Morpho and found its spiritual meaning to be associated with a broad and powerful representation of the soul and spiritual transformation. The blue color is often thought to symbolize healing, whether it is for personal healing or the healing of someone close to you.

A few days later another good friend, Cindy Wheeler, gave me a unique holiday gift she purchased in England. I opened up the box to find four artificial Blue Morpho butterflies that looked real. Again, I began to weep the minute I saw them. The tears came out of nowhere.

Neither Liz nor Cindy knew about my past-life regression and my seeing the Blue Morpho butterflies, yet here they both were, synchronistically delivering messages to me from the Divine.

Like the green and purple hearts, the Blue Morpho butterflies started coming at me full force and were always accompanied with instantaneous, deep-felt tears. Was I healing myself from past lives with all my tears? How deep from within me the tears came. If one doesn't heal from within, one can't help others, so each time it happened to me, a weight was being removed from my soul. My many tears along the way were not a sign of weakness, as I had always thought, but a sign of strength. I began to see a tapestry of my journey developing. All the dark and painful areas of my life were being intertwined with the light and joyful areas using a finely woven thread. It was my heart's pilgrimage to inherit what was rightly mine from the Divine Source. Not just mine alone, but for those who picked up their staff and followed.

🦋🦋🦋🦋🦋

As I continued to attend seminars, my desire was leaning more towards the end-of-life events for those preparing to leave the Earth Plane. I also wanted to learn more about NDE events that help to raise the thin veil between this life and the other side for a glimpse of the beauty that is to come.

The Wholelife Expo in Schaumberg, Illinois, featured Eben Alexander, and I sat in with many other interested attendees who wanted to hear about his NDE. Listening to him speak was even more fascinating than reading his book. Eben was able to peel the typed words he shared in his book right off the pages and bring them to life in the filled conference room. He created a visual canvas with his clear and concise spoken words for all to see and experience through his own heart.

At a later date, I traveled to the National Louis University in Skokie, Illinois, to hear Eben Alexander discuss his explorations of sound meditation and heart activation. He shared his belief in oneness and interconnectedness, and it was resonating with me. This was the battle cry I had been hearing and experiencing, and I wanted to explore more of it with others of like thinking.

My book collection was growing by leaps and bounds. My appetite to read as much as I could on these subjects was voracious. I had enough books to open a library of my own. In a way I did. I started lending out books to people I thought would benefit from reading them based on conversations we had. At times, I lost track of where my books were or whom I had given them to. It didn't matter to me. I had already read them, and they were meant for someone else's heart and soul.

The conference that turned the light on for me, and made me turn the corner, was with David Kessler, a death and grieving expert. He was a student of Elisabeth Kübler-Ross, known for her study of the five stages of death. Later, David co-wrote books with her on death and dying and on grief and grieving. His *Needs of the Dying* book was praised by Mother Teresa, and she summoned him to India regarding the words within his book.

His newest book being promoted at this particular seminar was *Visions, Trips, and Crowded Rooms: Who and What You See Before You Die*, which resonated powerfully within me. I have passed this book on to many people dealing with loved ones who were holding on for long periods of time before letting go of the Earth Plane. The responses from the families, both verbal and in the form of thank-you notes, overflowed with heartfelt gratitude.

My learning to not fear death during my first hot-stone massage event pushed me to want to understand more about how other people viewed death, prepared for it, welcomed it, or feared it. My desire to learn as much as I could on the subject was insatiable. The attraction was so intense, I realized the Divine Source was speaking to me and pushing me in this direction.

I wanted others to experience the need to release the fear of dying and see it as a journey of transition. First, we were babies, and then we were toddlers. We continued to grow through our teens and into adulthood. Most of us breezed right through each of those transitions, and more often than not, we never even noticed just precisely when or how they actually happened. To be able to help others approach death as another transition from our life cycle to returning to our Divine Source light cycle without holding onto the burden of fear became my most heartfelt wish for everyone.

I wanted those transitioning to feel they were never alone. If it is us, a family member on the Earth Plane at their side, or those that come as spirits from the spiritual realm to journey back with them. We are all beautiful, loving beings of light. We are stars shining brightly as we return to our Divine Source of energy and love.

Those left behind on the Earth Plane are never alone either, even though many close the door and see death as an absolute ending. The light of the soul that leaves our Earth Plane is never very far from us.

Take time to be still, and you'll experience them through the loving memory held in your own heart. Maybe a butterfly will land on your arm shortly after your loved one has passed and stays with you longer than usual. Your heart will skip a beat at that very moment to let you know it is your loved one. You may have a dream that is like no other you have ever experienced and your loved one will be in it speaking to you, holding you, or dancing with you. You will know the difference between this distinctive dream and any others you have ever had. It will be seared into the memory of your heart. You won't forget even the minutest detail of your dream. Your heart will hold it in its cellular memory forever. You'll remember what was said to you and the colors in your dream will be the most vibrant you have ever experienced.

During the day, you might see a red cardinal, a bird your loved one cherished, come to your breakfast nook window often to make sure you understand and hear it. Don't let anyone tell you, "It's just your imagination." You will know it's your loved one bringing you a message because your heart will have that special quickening within it that will radiate throughout your entire body. Hold on to the communications you are given and be grateful you were in tune to receive them. When it's all rolled up into one beautiful gift package, it's the bringing of Heaven and Earth together through the Divine Source that resides in all our hearts.

My understanding of the beauty of one's passing can be compared to the caterpillar transitioning itself into its protective chrysalis stage, and then finally into its crowning glory and ability to fly and be free.

🦋🦋🦋🦋🦋

At 3:15 a.m. I woke up and saw a beautiful cherub baby floating on its back in midair with eyes closed. I sat up on the edge of my bed to continue observing it. A bright white satin cloth was loosely wrapped around its waist and legs and gently flowed out beyond its feet. Shortly after, the vision slowly faded away. I settled back into bed and wondered what this vision meant, and tried to understand what I had just seen. I fell asleep not having any answers.

While getting ready for work in the morning, I continued to wonder about the vision. Could a baby mean a new beginning of some sort for me? If it was, what would that be? I would just have to wait and be patient. I had learned in the past, whatever vision I experienced in color would happen in the future.

I arrived at work and noticed Robin Lizowski, a co-worker, had not shown up on time for work. She wasn't scheduled to travel for the week, and she was always prompt about starting work on time. As an administrative assistant for our team group, I was to inform our senior manager whenever an employee from our group was over an hour late without notice. I was scheduled to attend an early morning meeting and would not know if Robin came in or not within that hour timeline or not until I got out from my meeting.

Upon returning to my workstation after my meeting, I checked and saw Robin was still not at her desk. I sought out the senior manager, who was talking to another employee around the corner from Robin's office. I came around the corner and stopped, and the senior manager saw me and asked, "Do you need something?"

I replied, "Have you heard from Robin?"

The senior manager replied back, "Yes, but I can't talk about it."

I replied, "No problem, I'm just glad you heard from her." I turned and took two steps and stopped. I turned back around and faced towards the senior manager. She noticed me and asked, "Do you need something else?"

I quietly mouthed the words, "She lost the baby."

I saw the senior manager's mouth drop open in disbelief. She responded with only a nod of her head to indicate yes. I turned around to leave, and the right side of my body fell up against the wall as my knees went weak. I was shocked by what I had said and when I was able to right myself, I quickly returned to my workstation and wept.

I didn't know where those words came from that left my mouth to go directly to the senior manager's ears. This wasn't the first time something like this had happened to me. Each time it occurred I was always reminded of what Donna Marie Levy told me, *"That you will be able to say what others cannot."*

About 20 minutes later, the senior manager came into my workstation and asked very directly, "Did you know Robin was pregnant?"

I replied, "No."

The look on the senior manager's face told me she didn't believe me. She turned sharply and left to go back to her office.

I found it hard to concentrate for the rest of the day thinking about Robin. I was also struggling with the thought my boss did not believe me. I went home and tossed around the idea of going in early to work the next day and sitting down with my boss and telling her what I had seen during the early morning hours. I had never talked to any of my team members about any of the things that were happening to me. Yet, I didn't want my boss to think I was lying to her.

I arrived early at work the next day and went into the senior manager's office, gently closing the door behind me. I was apprehensive about telling her anything. I wasn't sure how she would take it, much less understand it, without a lot of background detail, which I wasn't prepared to share. When I told her what I had experienced before coming to work the day before, I also wanted to make sure she knew I did not lie to her about not knowing Robin was pregnant.

The senior manager replied, "I know you didn't lie. I called Robin and asked her. Robin said she hadn't even told her family." On the one hand, I was relieved she knew I didn't lie to her, but on the other, I hurt inside knowing she needed to call Robin and find out for herself.

Robin returned to work the next week. She came into my workstation and sat down and asked, "Can you tell me what the baby looked like?" I was startled by her request because I didn't know the senior manager shared my vision with her. I relayed the details of what I had seen, and we both cried together.

Robin told me she was struggling with the loss and didn't really want to be at work. I said to her, "I do Reiki and if you'd like me to do it for you, let me know. I'll be happy to set some time aside for you."

She replied, "I'll think about it."

The next day, Robin again came into my workstation and asked, "Are you still willing to do Reiki for me?"

I replied, "Absolutely. What made you decide to have it done?"

She replied, "I never heard of Reiki, but I did some checking on it and decided I'd like to try it."

We set a date for after work, later in the week.

When Robin arrived for her Reiki session, we hugged, and she was still tearful and emotionally raw. I made her as comfortable as possible on the massage table and covered her with my quilted Reiki comforter with hearts stitched into it. When the hour session was up, Robin sat upright on the massage table and asked, "What does it mean to see all the colors of the rainbow? I saw an old-fashioned washboard floating in front of me, and all the rungs of the washboard were individual colors of the rainbow."

I replied, "With my experience of working with Reiki and colors, to me it represents someone who was on the earth for the first time, and I also equate the rainbow colors as messages from loved ones, especially children. Robin, I believe your baby was with you in your heart to let you know all is okay."

Robin was quiet and reflective as she took more time to sit quietly on the massage table and absorb what she had seen and what I had just told her. I gave her water to drink, and when she left for the evening, she was in a much calmer state of mind. We hugged goodbye without any tears.

🦋🦋🦋🦋

I began to notice numbers showing up on a regular basis. I'd look at my watch, or at the clock on the wall at work, or the clock in the car, or my alarm clock at home, and the same numbers showed up. I remembered my father in his later years telling Mom and me he always saw the number 111. He would even show us when it happened if we were around. He was amazed at how regularly it happened to him, and he would ask Mom and me, "Do you know what it means?" Mom and I didn't have a clue at the time.

Now I saw that same number, 111, along with others, on a regular basis, such as 222, 333, and 444. I began to read Doreen Virtue's book *Healing with the Angels: How the Angels Can Assist You in Every Area of Your Life*. There is a section in her book that discusses what these numbers mean. Doreen teaches that numbers are ways the angels can communicate with us if we are open to it.

Doreen later authored another quick reference book titled *Angel Numbers 101* that contains the angelic meanings of all numbers from 0 to 999. The ready reference book found an honorary place on my bedroom nightstand because the numbers started showing up on a consistent basis during the early morning hours. I would wake up and see the numbers on my alarm clock and then go back to sleep. After a while, I realized it was happening too regularly, so I started to keep track, and I always paid attention to the consistent messages the numbers represented.

I continued to deal with the intense feelings and nudges I was getting to be doing something other than my daily nine-to-five job. I asked for guidance, and most often these numbers kept coming up on a regular basis:

- 111 *told me to keep positive thoughts because my thoughts are manifesting instantly, so keep your mind set focused on your desires. Give any fearful thoughts to Heaven for transmutation.*
- 222 *told me to trust that everything was working out exactly as it's supposed to with Divine blessings for everyone involved. Let go and have faith.*

- *333 said I was completely surrounded, protected, loved and guided by the benevolent ascended masters.*
- *444 told me there are angels—they're everywhere around you! You are completely loved, supported, and guided by many Heavenly beings, and you have nothing to fear.*

The numbers changed from time to time, and soon I consistently saw:

- *777 told me I was definitely on the right path in every area of my life. To stay balanced and spiritually aware so that I could continue moving forward on this illuminated path.*
- *888 told me this was a very auspicious sign of complete financial support from the Universe. Money is flowing in my direction.*
- *904 told me God and the angels are supporting me as I focus on serving a spiritual purpose in this world.*

These were some pretty powerful messages, yet I didn't know where they would be leading me. Even though I continued to feel the nudges and the longing for something else I was supposed to be doing, I just couldn't see it yet.

❧❧❧❧

Mom and Dad were now both in their nineties and within a few years of each other, they both had to go into a nursing home facility. It was hard to see them go, but safety and care were a priority with their health situations. Both were in a nursing facility 30 minutes away from Sun Prairie. Since I was working, I visited them on weekends, and this left me with an empty nest to come home to every evening after work.

I'm not one to sit around, so I started to look into volunteering with hospice patients. I took on three patients located ten minutes away from my home. The hospice patients were each so special and unique, and I cherished the time I had to spend with them. I always seemed to connect well with older people all my life, so it was a good fit to work with my three new assignments. They all helped to fill a void in my life, and I hoped I brought some much-needed companionship into theirs.

One individual loved to have fresh flowers in her room, and I brought flowers as often as I could. She also loved to watch her *Wheel of Fortune* television show. There could be no talking during the show itself, except when she asked if I knew the answer. She prided herself on getting the answer before the contestants did, even if she had a little help from me. If we were able to beat the contestant, she would wait with great anticipation to see just how much fantasy money she had won. I never asked her for a cut of the action.

Another person I helped liked to receive big hugs when I arrived and when I left. She also loved to watch cooking shows and talk about the ingredients being used. I never had time to watch cooking shows while I was working, so I was picking up some great ideas as we watched together. I honestly believed she imagined how every spice and dish they prepared would taste to her. She could no longer eat these foods, but her memory and love for them were alive and well. She even suggested additional ideas to add her special touch to the dish being prepared that the professional chef had not used. I would tell her, "I gain ten pounds just watching the show with you."

My third hospice resident was a male. He loved symphony music, and I would bring in CDs for us to listen to because I too enjoyed it. We talked about history, which is another love of mine, and he taught me so much because he had come over from Germany at the age of 15, on his own, after World War II.

He let me know he didn't believe anything was waiting for us after we die. He didn't accept there was a Heaven or a Hell. We'd talk about it, since I thought there was, and he always ended each of our conversations with, "You believe what you want to believe, and I'll believe what I want to believe." We would both smile and laugh each time he said it.

He took ill and had to go to the hospital for a week. When he returned to the nursing home, I came to visit him. He was sitting in a wheelchair in the middle of the great room where everyone gathered outside their own private rooms. When I came in, and he saw me, I said, "What are you up to today?"

He replied, "I'm just sitting here waiting to go to Hell."

I sat down in front of him and said, "You told me you didn't believe in anything after we die."

He replied, "There must be that at least."

I made a deal with him, "Whichever one of us goes first will have to come back and let the other know if there is anything."

He replied with a smile and said, "Deal."

One week later at 3:00 a.m. on a Sunday morning, I woke up feeling a gentle hand on my left shoulder. I had never experienced anything like this before, and wondered what it could be. Later that day, I received a phone call from my hospice supervisor advising me my male hospice resident had passed away. I asked what time, and it coincided with the time I had felt the hand on my left shoulder. I think of him often and hope he is happy in his new and unexpected place of peace and he has the freedom and ability to fly and be free as a butterfly. My time with my three hospice residents lasted one year.

※ ※ ※ ※ ※

As things were happening to me and I became more aware of spiritual things happening around me, I started to recite a daily mantra on my way to work each morning. It started out small and grew to include more spiritual beings, and the most current mantra is, "Good morning, angels, archangels, masters, ascended masters, spiritual guide Sarah, guardian angel Martha, Holy Mary, Mother of God, the Holy Trinity, God the Father, Son, and Holy Spirit. Thank you for a beautiful day." This became the daily rain-or-shine mantra because every day was gorgeous. I affectionately called them my Celestial Team.

Through the years, the friends I had developed also started to share special spiritual events happening to them. Some stayed quiet for many years, but the more I shared my experiences, the more they came forth with theirs.

I was once told I shouldn't talk about these things, yet I believed my experiences were so intense because they were a part of me. If I couldn't talk about them, then I didn't need to be with those who didn't want to hear. When something comes from heartfelt love, I wanted to share it with as many as I could. I wanted the doors of their hearts to fly open and let the Divine Source show them what it can do for all of us.

As friends, we all decided to put together a small spiritual group where we could share our mystical experiences, and read books and discuss our findings. We also attended some seminars I previously mentioned together. Our assemblage traveled back and forth from my place in Sun Prairie to the home of Bob and Diane Reinen, and Gary and MaryAnn Dennis in DeForest, and Liz Awe in Greenfield, Wisconsin, and to Carolyn Awe in Hainesville, Illinois, depending on whose turn it was to have the monthly meeting. It was as if there was a universal magnet that brought all our lives together for whatever synchronistic reasons. There is something to be said about, "Likes attract."

❅❅❅❅❅

"For where two or three gather in my name,
there am I with them."
—Matthew 18:30 NIV

Chapter Eight
St. Germain Times Three

*"Make friends with the angels, who though invisible
are always with you. Often invoke them, constantly praise them,
and make good use of their help and assistance in all
your temporal and spiritual affairs."*
—Saint Francis De Sales

Spring had pushed out the bitter cold winter winds of Wisconsin and melted the last of our snow for the year. Summer was inching up behind, and I was looking forward to the warm breezes it would bring. That is, whenever it would reach us. June in Wisconsin can be very iffy when it comes to weather. Along Lake Michigan, it can stay cool until July depending on the prevailing winds. The same goes for Northern Wisconsin. If you plan a Wisconsin vacation in June, you best be prepared for all kinds of weather possibilities.

I was yearning for a change, something that would take me out of the hustle and bustle of the fast-moving world we are living in. I longed for peacefulness, beauty, and nature. I wanted to interact with humans, even if it was just a good morning or hello with a smile. I didn't want the negative daily news bombarding my very being every hour of every day. Nor did I want to hear my work computer "ding" to let me know I had more emails to add to the already growing mountain.

My heart guided me to what we call *God's Country* in Northern Wisconsin.

🦋 🦋 🦋 🦋 🦋

I decided to take an early vacation in June. If weather permitted, I wanted to read a good book and spend some time soaking up some much-needed sunshine on a sparkling blue lake. I found a resort in St. Germain, Wisconsin, that fit all my expectations. The resort had year-round homes and cottages along with a mom-and-pop bar/restaurant on the premises. The establishment would be perfect if I wanted to mingle with those staying at the resort, as well as those living in St. Germain, to get a flavor of the area.

I chose a three-bedroom cottage—two more bedrooms than I needed—so I asked my good friends Bob and Diane Reinen if they would like to join me for the week. We were all on the same page about wanting something simple and relaxing. Much to my delight, they were open to coming along. Their dog Jack was able to join us as well. Jack was a rock-hard black pug with an attitude to go with it. I called Jack a walking Sherman tank. Jack was small in stature, but strong as an ox and had a ebony coat of fur that glistened in the sunlight. I looked forward to having Jack with us.

St. Germain was three hours north of Sun Prairie. It was just far enough north to enjoy the incredibly tall, green pine trees and sparkling blue inland lakes to help forget about the outside world. The town of St. Germain was centrally located if we wanted to connect with the outside world for a day of shopping or an evening out for dinner. Eagle River was 13 miles to the east, and Minocqua was 17 miles to the southwest should the need arise.

We picked the third week of June for our resort reservation. As we drove through St. Germain, we observed a craft fair going on and a billboard announcing a free evening concert to start off the town's many summer events. All three of us were interested in checking it out after we settled into our cabin.

We arrived at our destination and checked out the lay of the land. Our cabin faced the lake and gave us easy access to the water's sandy beach. The lower level of the cottage was built into the hillside and was accessible from the main floor by a spiral staircase. The main floor of the cabin was high above the water. One of the bedrooms faced the lake and had windows on three sides of the room. If you rested on the bed, you only saw 180 degrees of water and tall pine tree tops. It gave you a feeling of being Huck Finn slowly floating down the river on his raft. Bob and Diane took the bedroom with the 180-degree view. I took the back bedroom on one condition—I have Jack at night in my room. I wanted Bob and Diane to have a restful time, and I also wanted to be able to take Jack out in the morning for his morning constitutional, while Bob and Diane got to sleep in.

Our first day of vacation was overcast and chilly. Upon arrival at the craft fair and the free concert in the park, Mother Nature decided to add some cold, drizzling rain for a touch of June ambiance in Wisconsin. Bob decided to check out the wood-carving displays while Diane and I checked out the craft booths, and we found a vendor selling handmade Reiki jewelry. I discovered a Reiki necklace with seven colored stones, each vertically wrapped with silver wire. Diane liked it, too, so we each bought the last two available. They would be our treasured finds from our week in St. Germain.

We all listened to part of the free concert and decided to go back to the cottage to warm up and dry out. We sat down in the dining room to play a card game of Royal Rummy for pennies and kept track of our winnings for the entire week. The weather for our vacation week was not the best, so we looked forward to playing cards and sitting down and breaking each other's piggy bank with our high-financed game of pennies while the rain danced on the cottage rooftop. We all braved the weather elements and bundled up to walk over to the mom-and-pop watering hole to meet the owner and end our evening with a nightcap before settling in for the night.

I took Jack out the first morning, and the weather was gray and overcast with a low-hanging fog. As Jack and I walked down the road to explore his new surroundings, a shadow came over the top of us. I immediately stopped and looked up and didn't see anything due to the fog, but my instinct told me it wasn't normal. Jack finished his morning duty, and I hurried him back to the cottage. I mentioned the incident to Bob at breakfast, and he advised me there were eagles on the lake. Bob suspected one may have swooped low to check on us, especially Jack. Jack was small, but he was a massive tank when it came to weight. I didn't think the eagle would win if he decided to have Jack for a snack. The rest of the week, I walked Jack each morning and watched the sky above us at all times with my keen hawk eyes for any winged invaders.

Midweek, the weather cleared, and we rented a pontoon boat for the day. Bob was our chief navigator as he took us around the entire lake and then let the pontoon boat float along on its own for the rest of the day as we all relaxed, read books and soaked up the warm sunshine. That afternoon time stood still for me as I immersed myself in the sounds of nature and the beauty of the Northwoods surrounding us.

There was a new A-frame home across from our cottage. The people using it had left for the day, so Diane and I walked over to check out the property and peek inside the front window. It was a two-story home with all modern appliances and furniture. We went back and told Bob about it, and all of us were interested in finding out if it would be available for rent the next summer. We inquired about the A-frame's availability and got our name on the resort calendar for the following June, only this time we would take the last week in June, hoping for better weather.

Our week in God's Country passed by too quickly. We returned home well rested, which is what Diane and I needed before having to return to our crazy work schedules. Bob was already checking into weekly pontoon rentals for the next year since all of us wanted a pontoon we could keep at our resort dock to be used at a moment's notice. Bob became our social director, and he looked into additional areas of interest for us to explore the next year.

❦ ❦ ❦ ❦ ❦

The following year brought three unexpected changes for all of us. Dad was slowly drifting away in his mind. Some days were good, and others were not. It was like riding a roller coaster watching him go through his high and low days.

Dad had celebrated his 90th birthday in March a year earlier, and we invited family and friends to share in the celebration at his nursing home. All my long-lost cousins came to the party, and I was pleasantly reunited, after 30 years, with my favorite cousin Bob Awe and his wife, Liz.

Bob, Liz, and I were able to reconnect on some occasions throughout the next year to rekindle our long overdue family connection. Even though there was a 30-year time span of not getting together, it felt like we had never been apart. We picked up right where we left off and moved forward with zest. Bob always told me I was his favorite cousin, and I had to agree; he too was my favorite. Little did I know Bob's time on the earth would be cut short that year with a serious illness.

My vacation pal Jack, a.k.a. the Sherman tank, was also put to sleep that same year.

※ ※ ※ ※ ※

When it came time for our second June trip to St. Germain, Bob, Diane, and I asked Liz if she would like to join us for a week away. She was grateful for the invite but unable to come because she was planning a wedding celebration for her son and new daughter-in-law that same week. We asked her to keep the same week next year open so she could join us, and she agreed.

During our second year at the resort, Bob, Diane, and I continued to play card games in the evening, and the winner had to buy a round of drinks at the end of the night at the on-site pub. We were on a first-name basis with the owners from the year before and felt like we were at home when welcomed back again this year.

We also became more familiar with the surrounding area of St. Germain by venturing out to nearby towns to investigate their shops and restaurants. We enjoyed having our own pontoon boat for the entire week so we could continue to float freely on the water, read more books, and soak up the warm sunshine whenever we wanted to.

We picked a good week for weather and were able to come back home with reasonable tans and again feel rested before having to return to the rat race of work. Before leaving the resort, we set up a rental schedule for the A-frame home for our third year with the same pontoon, and we again picked the last week in June.

❧ ❧ ❧ ❧ ❧

The third year in St. Germain was lots of fun. Liz joined us, and she was the keeper of the games. She taught all of us lots of dice cup games, additional card games, of which Hand and Foot became our favorite, and Mexican dominos just to name a few. Liz raised the stakes this third year from pennies to quarters, because she liked to sweeten the winning pot. We each brought along our own private bank of quarters. The winner of each evening game still had to pay for a round of drinks at the on-site pub. Laughter was a priority to enjoy all the games. We couldn't finish with our evening meal fast enough to get the table set up for our evening of fun. Neighbors sitting outside enjoying their campfires on the warm nights could hear our laughter, which drifted out through the opened screened doors of our A-frame.

We continued to enjoy the pontoon floating on the lake and reading our books. This year, Bob surprised all of us with pink shirts to wear as we drifted on the lake in our pontoon boat. Bob's shirt had "Skipper" printed on the front, Diane had "Skipper's Mate 1", Liz had "Skipper's Mate 1-1/4," and I had "Skipper's Mate 1-1/2." I bought matching wide-brimmed hats for the gals, and we gave Bob his skipper cap.

One afternoon, while floating leisurely on the lake, I saw something sticking up out of the water and approaching our pontoon from the distant shoreline. It was hard to make it out, but I wondered if we had Nessie in our lake. The creature kept coming closer to our boat, and I asked Bob to turn around from where he was sitting and see if he could tell me what was approaching. Bob could not determine what it was from his vantage point. We all continued to watch the creature, and as it came close enough to our pontoon, we could see it was a deer swimming across the lake. There had been construction going on along the distant shoreline, and it must have spooked the young deer into the water.

We watched as its head and ears were barely up out of the water as it struggled to get to the opposite shore. The approaching landscape consisted of a steady incline of rock and loose ground. There was no sandy shoreline on which the deer could rest before being able to get itself to protective cover in the trees higher up. We all watched helplessly as it struggled to climb out of the water onto the rocky incline. We were all feeling the pain and weakness of the animal, and when the deer was able to pull its body up and out of the water with its last burst of energy, it quickly disappeared into the trees. We all cheered with delight.

Each day, we watched the majestic eagles flying over the lake and catching their meals from just below the water line. Nature this year was giving us all a show, and we appreciated the front-row seats we had to take it all in. During the week we took a half-day nature tour and observed large blue herons perched high up on the branches of pine trees. We didn't think it was possible for them to balance that high up, but we all took pictures to prove it.

We were also able to see an eagle's nest that had fallen from a damaged tree along the shoreline. I had no idea how huge an eagle's nest could be. An average bald eagle nest can be four to five feet in diameter and two to four feet deep. Each year, the adult pair of birds adds another one to two feet of material to the nest. It was a magnificent work of art to see up close and personal.

❋ ❋ ❋ ❋ ❋

My book to read this vacation week was titled *Wishes Fulfilled—Mastering the Art of Manifestation* by Dr. Wayne W. Dyer. I woke up early on Tuesday morning, before anyone else was up, and sat in the living room to read. The author was asking the reader, especially any Catholics reading his book, to keep an open mind as he wrote about an ascended master's "I AM" discourses.

Diane got up shortly after and came out into the kitchen, and she heard me giggling as I was reading my book. She asked, "What are you reading that is so funny?"

I replied, "Isn't it interesting that we are all in St. Germain, Wisconsin, on St. Germain Lake and I'm reading about an ascended master by the name of St. Germain?"

Diane sat down on the living room couch and googled Ascended Master St. Germain on her cell phone. She had never heard of him, and a picture came up of a man of slender build with a goatee beard. Diane began to read out loud about him, "He has appeared on the earth at different times as different people, and he is believed to have many magical powers, such as the ability to teleport, levitate, walk through walls, and to inspire people by telepathy." It didn't mean much to either of us, so Diane got up and made her breakfast, and I continued to read my book.

The plan for the day was to take a shopping expedition to Eagle River to check out the stores, have lunch, and return to the resort later in the day. Bob was our navigator on land and water, so he drove the three of us gals to Eagle River.

Just a few miles outside of Eagle River, Bob hit the car brakes hard, and we all became aware of a mother deer and her two fawns starting to cross the highway in front of our car. The animals stopped briefly in front of the vehicle, and all three looked directly at us as if saying, *"Thank you and welcome."* We all watched with delight as they continued to saunter across the highway and quickly disappear into the thick woods. It was an extraordinary moment to see two fawns with their mother. Nature was continuing to put on an upfront and personal show for all of us.

In Eagle River, Bob would go his own way to find things that interested him and Diane, Liz, and I would always meet up with him somewhere along the way. More often than not, Bob would locate us first because we were usually heavily involved in shopping. The three of us gals started to check out the stores on both sides of East Wall Street.

Liz was new to our group this year, and Diane and I soon found out she had radar when it came to finding jewelry stores. Liz was not able to pass by a jewelry store without stopping to look in the window or just go right into the store. We teased her about it, and we all had to admit she had a trained eye for a great deal. She was precise when it came to matching up her pieces of jewelry along with the art of haggling whenever it was appropriate. Diane and I watched and learned as Liz, the master, shopped for her jewelry and showed us how it was done.

Diane, Liz, and I were coming to the end of the business district on East Wall Street for downtown Eagle River. As we looked across the street, we saw an unusual old storefront painted pink with blue trim. Above the storefront window, we saw the name of the store, Pink Coyote. Our curiosity got the best of us, so the three of us started to cross the street to check out our last shop of the day. Our first impression of the storefront was a typical Northern Wisconsin tourist place. As we continued to cross the street, we saw that it contained Southwest Indian Art and Jewelry. Again, our first impression was it probably was a typical up-north tourist trap of trinkets and moccasins.

Much to our surprise and laughter as we entered the store, it was the most beautiful shop we had been in for the entire day and for any other year we had been in the area. Yes, it pleased Liz immediately—it had jewelry! I was intrigued when I saw the beautiful Indian handmade woven baskets, kachina dolls, peace pipes, and dream catchers, along with delicate hand-painted pottery. The store was set up beautifully with the different colored gemstones and their matching pieces. I immediately thought of the old saying, *"Don't judge a book by its cover."* The inside of the store was spacious and soft Native American flute music was playing in the background, which helped to lull us all further into the store to enjoy the beauty waiting for us to peruse.

Each area of the store told a story of the quality artwork displayed and handmade by many southwest Native American Indian tribes, including Hopi, Navajo, and Zuni. It gave me a feeling of being in a modern museum tended with loving care. This store was our last stop of the day, and by far our most significant treasure find of the entire week. Diane and I were never big into having a lot of jewelry, but today, all three of us were in search of our own individual piece of beauty.

The owner introduced himself to us as John LaBelle. I immediately wondered if he might be a distant relative, since my maternal grandmother's maiden name was LaBelle too. John had two Dachshund dogs in their carrying cages on the floor behind the jewelry counter keeping him company. John brought out the dogs to meet us, and they hurriedly scampered back into their cages for their afternoon naps. John was very accommodating, showing us different jewelry pieces and giving us the background history of the items and the artists who made them. Time stood still as we had the entire store to ourselves to immerse ourselves in this newly found treasure trove.

I saw Diane intently looking at rings that interested her in one part of the store, and I was drawn to the colored opals. John brought out a rack of opal rings from inside the glass case for me to look at and try on at my leisure. As I was deciding what I would pick, I sensed someone off to my right, standing close to me. I didn't see the person, but I knew there was someone very close. As I continued to look at the rings, I instinctively reached down on my right side and pulled my shoulder purse up and placed it in front of me on the counter. As soon as I did it, I instantly felt guilty and thought to myself, *"Why did I do that? I didn't have any reason to."* I had hoped the person standing close to me didn't notice what I had done.

Diane was standing just off to my left side. I decided to move to another area of the store, and as I turned, I saw a slenderly built man with light olive skin and a perfectly shaped goatee standing behind me. As I moved to the center of the room, I heard Diane ask the owner, John, a question about what seemed to be an imperfection in a stone of a ring she was interested in. At that very moment, the unknown man replied, "Indian artists purposely put a flaw in every piece of jewelry because nothing in nature is perfect."

Liz was standing to the back of the store checking on jewelry in another glass display that interested her, but she was also taking in everything that was happening and being said in the front of the store.

The unidentified man stated he was of Indian background. I walked over to him and said, "I too have Indian heritage. I was told it was Ojibwe." My pronunciation was with a long O the word *jib* with a soft *I* and ended with the sound of the word *way* with a long *a*. The unknown man immediately corrected me and said it was pronounced with an ending of *wa* with a soft *ah* sound. When he said it, it sounded more French to me. Since my maternal great-grandparents came from Quebec, Canada, it resonated correctly for me. I stepped over to the man and gently touched his arm and thanked him for the pronunciation correction.

Usually, when I speak to someone I always make eye contact, but this time I did not when I thanked this man. I was intrigued by his goatee and the delicate braid in its center. I had never seen anything like it, and I was distracted wondering how he could have possibly created this delicate and perfectly centered braid.

The mystery man moved towards the entrance of the store as if to leave and then turned around in the doorway to face us. He put both of his arms up with palms facing out toward us and spoke in his native tongue. Obviously, none of us understood a word he was saying, but the words rolled off his tongue melodically, and we all were part of something very unusual happening. As soon as he finished speaking, he stated, "I will translate for all of you. You are all three beautiful women." He then turned and walked out of the store.

I immediately turned toward the counter where the owner John was putting a ring tray back into the glass case. I asked, "John, do you know who that man was?" John never looked up but shook his head no. As fast as I questioned John, I turned toward the entrance of the store and saw Bob standing in the doorway. Bob had finally caught up with us. I immediately asked Bob, "Did you see the man who just walked out of the store?"

Bob replied, "There isn't anyone outside of the store or on the entire city block in either direction." We women didn't quite understand what we just experienced, but it made for an exciting day at the Pink Coyote. All three of us purchased jewelry pieces and then headed back to St. Germain with Bob.

The three of us shared with Bob our Pink Coyote experience during the ride back to the resort. Diane and I mentioned that the man looked very much like the picture that had come up on Diane's cell phone that morning when she looked up information on the Ascended Master St. Germain. Since Bob didn't see anyone on the block outside the store, we all thought the whole situation was just too bizarre. I teased Bob and said, "Bob, it was probably you. You were manifesting again." We arrived back at our resort and got ready for dinner, and did not talk about it the rest of the evening.

❄ ❄ ❄ ❄ ❄

One of the aftereffects of having been given three different chemotherapies when I had cancer, was that my female vulva area became painfully inflamed. I was told there was no medical cure for it. Going to the bathroom was always painful, and I had been living with this pain for twelve years.

Early the next morning, the day after our trip to Eagle River, around 3:00 a.m., I had to get up and use the bathroom. This morning, like every other time I used the bathroom, I prepared myself for the intense pain to come, but nothing happened. I couldn't believe it. I blew it off as a onetime "get-out-of-pain" card, and I accepted it gratefully. I returned to bed and again had to go to the bathroom at 5:30 a.m. I was given another "get-out-of-pain" card. I thought, *"This can't be!"*

Instead of going back to bed, I went downstairs to the living room and continued to read my book. I put the book down after a few pages of reading and thoughts started running through my mind about the day before. This was our third year vacationing in St. Germain. The day started with me giggling about the three St. Germains I told Diane about in the morning. I remembered the three deer stopping our car on the way into Eagle River and how all three of them looked at us. Was this nature's way of connecting and letting me know we needed to pay attention because something was going to mystically happen? I remembered us three gals having the entire Pink Coyote store to ourselves for the whole time we were there. I also recalled how I sensed someone standing next to me in the store, yet I did not see the person, nor did I hear the person come into the store.

The mystery man did three things while he was in the store. First, he answered a question about nature for Diane. Second, he corrected my pronunciation of Ojibwe and third, he paid all three of us a compliment by saying, "You are all three beautiful women." I realized I just wasn't paying attention to all of the "three" combinations of messages I had been shown all day long.

I anxiously waited for Diane to get up because she was the only one I had ever told about my twelve years of pain and what caused it. Diane was a nurse, and I wanted to ask her if she might know why I no longer had any pain.

Diane came out into the kitchen a few hours later, and I asked, "Diane, can you come and sit down with me for a moment. I have something I want to discuss with you and need your medical expertise." Diane sat down, and I told her what had happened at 3:00 a.m. and 5:30 a.m. She wasn't able to give me any logical reason why I didn't have any pain. We were whispering in the living room when Liz got up and walked into the kitchen to get her morning coffee.

Liz asked, "What are you guys talking about?"

I replied, "Liz, I'll explain it to you when we take our morning walk. I don't want Bob to come walking out and hear us talking about this subject." Liz didn't want to wait until the walk. She came over, and I explained to her my health situation and my pain-free morning.

Liz immediately replied, "I've got chills running through my body." I asked why?

She stated, "Kathy, you are the only one of us who reached out and touched the man's arm when you thanked him at the Pink Coyote."

We all looked at each other in disbelief. Could the man we encountered really have been the Ascended Master St. Germain whom we had talked about heading home from Eagle River? I continued to use my "get-out-of-pain" card from that day forward. Diane, Liz, and I continued to remind each other, with a smile, "We are all three beautiful women."

❈❈❈❈❈

During the next year, Dad turned 94 in March, and his health was continuing to decline. Old age was wearing him down and his body was slowly giving way. When I visited him, he had a habit of keeping his eyes closed when he sat in his wheelchair. It would be hard to tell if he was sleeping or just resting his eyes and listening to what was going on around him. Most often he was awake and quietly eavesdropping, and every now and then he would surprise us with an interjected response to a conversation. I could feed him at lunch, and he would not open his eyes. I would have to direct him to open his mouth to take the food, and he would respond like a baby bird. It was difficult to watch him slowly slipping away from the vibrant, healthy, interactive man I remembered him as.

Two months later, I received a phone call at work telling me Dad had been taken to the Emergency Room at the local hospital. I was told it wasn't anything life-threatening according to the nursing home staff. His catheter had become disconnected and had to be reinserted. I immediately left work and drove to the hospital to be with him. When I arrived, I was delighted to see Dad had his eyes wide open. I truly missed seeing his Paul Newman ice-blue eyes. I gave him a kiss and took his left hand into mine.

He immediately told me, "It will all soon be over, and I will be alone." I knew this trip to the Emergency Room was not life-threatening, so I replied, "Dad, when that time comes, I'll be with you." He then smiled back at me with what I called his Irish shit-eating grin. I hadn't seen that grin on his face for a very long time. At that moment, I realized Dad was sharing with me what he knew was coming. I was honored he shared it with me, mainly since I couldn't talk to him about my spiritual events and happenings through the years. How I wished I could have shared them with him like I was able to share them with Mom. Yet this moment in time made up for everything, as far as I was concerned. Dad knew, at that very moment, that I would understand exactly what he was saying to me.

The hospital advised me that it would not be possible to insert the catheter because there wasn't anyone available that day at the hospital to do it. I then had to make arrangements to have Dad transferred to a hospital in Madison for the procedure. I followed the ambulance to Madison. As Dad was being wheeled into the Emergency

Room by the EMTs, I was parking my car across the street in the hospital parking complex. As I walked up to the Emergency Room door entrance, I received a call from the ER nurse asking, "Where are you?"

I replied, "I'm just coming into the Emergency Room entrance now."

The nurse stated, "We are all done with your dad. You can return him to the nursing home." It really was a simple procedure, as long as you had the right staff on hand to handle it. Unfortunately for Dad, it took over four hours to get it done.

When the EMTs put Dad in the ER to be taken care of, they were directed by the ER staff to go down the hall and get coffee and treats before they returned to their base location because the hospital was honoring all EMT personnel that day. Typically, the ambulance service that delivers the patient does not wait to return the patient back to their point of origin.

As I walked into Dad's emergency room, the nurse again told me they were done with Dad's procedure. I was also advised I would have to make arrangements to get another ambulance to take Dad back to the nursing home. The two EMTs arrived back in Dad's ER room to recover their equipment for their return trip. When they knew Dad was already finished and ready to go back to the nursing home, they said they would take him. I was relieved I didn't have to start calling around for another ambulance service. Timing was everything!

I was standing at the base of Dad's ER bed when the EMT team was getting ready to move him onto their mobile equipment. Just before they touched Dad, he looked directly past my right shoulder, and bellowed out in the loud voice he was well known for, "Ma!"

I asked the ER nurse, "What are his vitals?"

The nurse had just taken off the blood pressure cuff and said, "Everything was showing up normal."

Dad again hollered out, "Ma!" I knew immediately his mother had paid him a visit from the other side. I was again grateful to be standing with him at that moment. I believe with all my heart that someone special comes for us when the time is near.

Each time Dad called out, the EMT team jumped because his voice was so loud and insistent. They then prepared Dad for his return trip to the nursing home, and I again followed along behind in my car. When we arrived at the nursing home, Dad grinned his special Irish grin at me as he was removed from the ambulance and taken back to his room. I stayed with him until he was settled in and had his evening meal brought to him.

Dad's room was located on one end of the wing and Mom's was on the opposite end. The entire wing was divided in the middle with a great room for family gatherings and having daily resident meals. Mom and Dad spent a lot of time together in the great room each day. Before leaving the nursing home, I went down to the great room to find Mom and stayed with her while she had her evening dinner. The nursing staff had told me they kept her busy during the day, so she wasn't aware of what Dad was going through and she would remain calm.

I drove back to Madison to my place of work and made up my time for being away from the office during the day. It had been a long day, and I arrived home in Sun Prairie that night at 11:00 p.m. I fell into bed and into an uninterrupted sleep. I never heard my phone ring during the early morning hours. The hospice nurse had left a message on my cell phone during the early morning hours telling me Dad's vitals were changing and that I should come back to the nursing home.

I didn't get the message until I woke up at my usual time in the morning to start getting ready for work. I hurried to get to the nursing home and every movement I made felt like I was in slow motion. It was as if something was purposely holding me back, yet I was fighting with all I had to get to him. When I arrived at the nursing home, I could see his favorite nurse standing outside his room crying. When I got up to her, she said, "Kathy, your dad has passed. You missed him by five minutes."

I asked her, "Was anyone in the room with Dad when he passed?"

She replied, "No, he was alone."

I realized everything Dad told me the day before had come to pass as he said it would. I also knew why I hadn't heard the telephone call during the night and why I felt I was being held back getting ready in the morning. I wasn't supposed to be there, nor was anyone else. Yes, he was alone on the Earth Plane when he passed over, but in my heart, I knew his loving mother was waiting to accompany him to the other side.

That same morning, Dad's favorite nurse told me the night before, they had looked all around for my mom to get her ready for bed and they weren't able to find her in her usual hangout places. When the staff exhausted all of the possible locations she could have been, they decided to check Dad's room, and they found her sitting in the dark next to his bed holding his hand. The nurse advised me Mom had never gone down the hall to Dad's room after the evening dinner hour for all the time she had been in the nursing home.

Mom wasn't able to speak due to her dementia, but she was aware of everything that was being said to her and what was going on around her. Mom and Dad had a beautiful, loving relationship, and when I heard this story, it was as if Dad had communicated heart-to-heart with her to let Mom know the end was coming soon.

❈ ❈ ❈ ❈ ❈

A week later, I arrived home from work about 7 p.m., and opened up a box of treasures that had belonged to Dad to prepare for his memorabilia table at his upcoming memorial service. I put the box on the kitchen table and pulled out a framed picture of Dad in his World War II blue Coast Guard jacket. I stood for a few moments thinking about how handsome he was and how beautiful his naturally wavy hair looked in the picture. I also thought, *"Boy, Mom sure knew how to pick a good-looking guy."* I put the picture down on the kitchen table and turned to my left to see the floor lamp standing in the corner of the living room had gone on all by itself. I thought it strange at the time, but it continued to come on at different times during the evening hours for months after Dad had passed. Often, I would be sitting in a chair reading a book across the room from the floor lamp and the light would go on. After a number of these events happened, I walked over to the floor lamp and cupped my hands around the pole. The energy I felt was intense. If I turned the light off and then turned it back on by myself, I wasn't able to experience the same intense energy. Since it had started the night I was looking at Dad's picture, I came to know I was being paid a visit. I would always say, "Hi, Dad. I love you," and leave the light on until I retired for the evening.

My "Doubting Thomas" persona moved the floor lamp to different rooms to see if the same thing would happen and it did. I realized Dad was making his presence known; although not in body, he was here in energy.

❧❧❧❧❧

A month after Dad's memorial service, I had a vivid dream of him.

He was in his early thirties, and was wearing a beautiful white suit. I could see Mom sitting in the background, and I sensed he was letting me know her time would soon follow. As we looked at each other, he put his right arm out in front of him with all five fingers pointing directly at me, and he sprayed me with a bright color orange from his fingers.

I immediately woke up and sat on the end of the bed. I wrote in my journal what I had seen. I noticed a light glowing in the hallway area, so I walked through the bedroom toward the hallway, and I could see the floor lamp in the living room was on. The floor lamp had only gone on in the evening hours after I came home from work. It had never come on during the night after I went to bed. I stood in amazement to see it lit as tears ran down my face. They were happy tears and tears of understanding. I went over to the floor light and again cupped my hands around the pole and felt the strong surge of energy. I thanked Dad for coming to me, and I understood his message about spraying me with bright orange.

The orange color in the vision was more brilliant than I had ever seen before. In Reiki, orange represents the sacral area, and it also has to do with having the ability to give to and receive from others on all levels of creativity. I had been journaling all my spiritual experiences for many years because others said I should, but at that moment, I knew I would also be writing about them.

❅ ❅ ❅ ❅ ❅

Seven months later, I had Darcy Lutzow and Judy Broman over for dinner. I had told them after Dad passed away about the floor lamp going on by itself. They were aware of it but hadn't experienced it. While the three of us were sitting at the table enjoying our evening dinner, the light went on. The floor lamp was directly behind Darcy, so when I noticed it I told her, "Darcy, turn around."

As she turned and saw the light, she immediately replied, "Hi Bill, its Tillie!" Tillie was the Irish nickname Dad had given to Darcy the first time he met her.

❅ ❅ ❅ ❅ ❅

"There are different kinds of gifts, but the same Spirit distributes them. There are different kinds of service, but the same Lord. There are different kinds of working, but in all of them and in everyone it is the same God at work."
—1 Corinthians 12:4-6 NIV

Chapter Nine
One's Purpose

"Let yourself be drawn by the stronger pull
of that which you truly LOVE."
—Rumi

A few months after my favorite cousin Bob Awe passed away, his wife Liz invited me to join her for dinner at a restaurant in Milwaukee. During our dinner, Liz told me how she and Bob had planned to spend their 40th wedding anniversary in the Hawaiian Islands. Even though Bob was no longer here, Liz still wanted to honor their anniversary plans by making the trip, and she wondered if I would like to join her.

The invitation was unexpected, and I was honored that she asked me. I immediately wondered what islands Liz wanted to go to because I had always wanted to go to Oahu to see Pearl Harbor. When I asked, Liz stated she wanted to go to Maui and Kauai. I wondered if she would be willing to add a third island into the mix so I could see Pearl Harbor and she was open to it. Three islands it would be!

✕✕✕✕✕

Liz had been having some vivid dreams of Bob after his passing, and she had shared them with me. I asked Liz if she would like to have a reading with a well-known psychic/spiritual counselor named Kathleen Schneider from Middleton. Liz was open to having a reading, so I set it up. I also arranged to have a reading for myself as well.

I had met Kathleen years earlier during my high "Doubting Thomas" era. The first time I let her do a reading for me, I didn't give her anything to work with. No upfront questions, no body language or facial changes to give away any of my thoughts, and no jewelry for her to hold. To alleviate any skepticism I had, she needed to prove to me how good she was.

Kathleen proceeded to knock me off my chair for my first reading. During her readings, she is able to share things from the past, present, and potential future. For the past, she told me, "Your maternal great-grandfather died of a blow to the head, and it wasn't his fault."

My mother had told me years before this reading that my maternal great-grandfather was a pugilist and he would never fight outside of the boxing ring. Townspeople would taunt him to try to get him to fight, and he always refused. One day, a man was attempting to provoke him, and then the man took a swing at him and hit him in the head. He died instantly.

For the present, Kathleen told me, "Your brother Michael was only here on the earth for a short time. He knew it would be for a short time before he came to the earth. His time here was a lesson.

For Kathleen to name my brother was an immediate shock to me. Michael had only lived nine months and died during a surgical procedure to repair his cleft pallet. It wasn't until 40 years later that my mother told me she and Dad had received a letter from the attending surgeon shortly after Michael's death. The surgeon explained to them how profoundly Michael's death affected him, and he was leaving his practice in Milwaukee to work as a doctor for the poor in the islands of the Pacific.

For the potential future, Kathleen told me she saw me sitting under a picture of a sea captain with a pipe in his mouth, and he is facing to the right of me.

I had already been to Ireland a few years before with Darcy, and I already had a photo of me sitting under a picture of a sea captain smoking his pipe and facing to the right of me just as Kathleen had described. I broke my silence and told Kathleen, "I have already done this." Kathleen replied, "You will be returning to Ireland."

ꖶ ꖶ ꖶ ꖶ ꖶ

Liz and I arrived in Middleton on a sunny Saturday morning in October for our readings with Kathleen. Liz went first while I waited in the reception room for the next hour. I approached my second reading with Kathleen with more respect and no skepticism. I told Kathleen at the beginning of our meeting how I had handled my first reading with her and how her reading affected me. I wanted her to know my thoughts had taken an entirely different perspective since I last met her. Kathleen was grateful for my sharing this with her.

For this reading, I brought my *Gate of Light* necklace so Kathleen could do psychometry, and I also brought along my journal with the vision entry of the geometric figure just in case I needed to confirm anything. I didn't tell Kathleen I was bringing my journal or anything about the necklace. I had the journal in a bag and placed it on the floor next to my chair.

Kathleen held the *Gate of Light* necklace in the palm of one hand and rubbed her other hand over the top of it. She said, "I see the number nine all around it. You are going to receive nine gifts." I shared with Kathleen my journal vision/drawing of the geometric figure with the nines in all of the spaces. It was my way of affirming that she was dead on.

Kathleen then told me, "You will be taking a trip with Liz, and you will be going to the Hawaiian Islands. You will be going home on this trip. You will feel comfortable when you arrive."

I was surprised she mentioned the trip and then wondered if Liz might have brought it up in her reading before me, so I asked, "Did Liz mention the trip in her reading with you?" Kathleen replied that Liz hadn't.

When Liz and I arrived at the Oahu airport, we walked to the outside of the terminal to wait for a driver who would be coming from our hotel to transport us and others who were going to the same hotel. When the driver arrived, she exited the van and walked towards our waiting group. She came directly up to me and looked me in the eyes, and quietly said, "Welcome home." I was stunned. Liz, standing next to me, heard her say it and poked me in the arm and asked, "Did you hear what she said?" I shook my head yes. Liz remembered what I shared with her about my reading with Kathleen back in October.

As the driver greeted the others waiting for a ride to the hotel, she did not welcome anyone else "home."

Kathleen had told me, "You and Liz will have tickets for something while on this trip that will be beyond thrilling for you."

While staying in Ka'anapali, on the island of Maui, Liz and I bought tickets for whale watching in Lahaina, just off of Front Street. This area is on the west side of the island. The whale-watching season in Maui goes from late September to mid-May, and the peak time for whale watching was in February and March. Liz and I arrived in February to take in this yearly birthing and mating ritual for the humpback whales coming from the cold waters of Alaska to the West lee of the island for the warmest and calmest waters needed for the whales to birth and mate.

We decided not to take a large tour boat but opted instead to acquire the small eight-man rubber raft with a female captain and male guide who had also previously worked with the Pacific Whaling Foundation on Maui.

The day was overcast and windy, and the waves were choppier than usual. My daredevil instinct told me the rubber raft was the way to go. I love things that go fast. Liz, on the other hand, does not like to be in water where her feet can't touch the bottom. This excursion was going to go beyond her comfort zone, and I was grateful she was willing to take a chance and go for the gusto. She proceeded to down a pill to prevent motion sickness.

There was a couple nearby, on the boat dock, debating if they should buy tickets for the raft or go with the larger boat due to the size of the waves. I overheard them and kiddingly replied to them, "Come on. The rubber raft ride will be a trip of a lifetime." They bought their tickets for the raft.

All passengers left their shoes and sandals in a box on the dock and boarded the raft barefooted. We sat in the middle of the raft. Four passengers sat on one side on a flat bench, and the other four sat on the other side with our backs to each other.

The young couple debating whether or not to take this ride sat next to me. The husband informed me he was an independent photographer hoping to get some good photos of the whales.

The captain maneuvering our raft was able to make the raft skip effortlessly across the top of the waves. It felt like we were flying just above the waves as we headed out to find the visiting whales. The way she skillfully handled the raft made me wonder if she had been a Navy Seal. The faster we went, the more I liked it, but we also needed to secure ourselves to stay seated on our flat benches. Liz and I decided to tuck our bare feet up and under the rope that was tightly woven around the entire outside portion of the rubber raft, to firmly hold us in place.

The waves and wind created a wash of water that left everyone on the raft soaked to the bone. It was enjoyable because the water was as warm as bath water. We were letting our inner child come out and enjoyed every minute of this experience.

The independent photographer sitting next to me had to secure his camera and forget about trying to get any pictures due to the weather and water conditions. Photos obtained while on the raft would be with our mind's eye only.

The whales were in abundance and, when spotted by our guide, our raft was the first to the scene. We watched the larger boats in the distance struggling to turn in different directions to get to the action due to their size. The choice we made to take the raft was the right one.

We saw the whales breach the water with ease and grace; we saw and heard them thunderously slap their tails on the surface of the water, and we were able to get as legally close as possible, up to 100 yards away, to watch baby calves swim with their mothers.

The whole morning on the raft was a breathtaking event. Just when I thought it couldn't get any better than this, the captain suddenly killed the motor of the raft. Our guide became very excited and quickly moved to the side of the raft and stretched his body out as far as he could over the edge to see something under the water. He loudly proclaimed, "Hang on! A whale is coming toward us and going directly under our raft." My heart was beating with absolute exhilaration. To be this close and one with nature was beyond thrilling for me.

When we arrived back at the boat dock, we all reclaimed our shoes and sandals from the waiting box on the pier. The independent photographer came up to me and thanked me for talking him and his wife into a thrill of a lifetime.

Before leaving Maui, Liz and I took a drive along the Honoapiilani coastal highway. Along the way, there was a high cliff of rocks that blocked our view of the bright blue ocean on the right side of the road. While driving, I was able to see up ahead where the rocky cliff would end, and we would again be able to see the beautiful blue water. As the rocky cliff gave way, I also saw a parking area crowded with cars. I made an unannounced sharp right turn off the highway and pulled into a large lookout parking area. Liz was holding on for dear life as I made the turn and wondered what was happening. As I entered the lookout area the lot was completely full of cars except for one open space directly in front of us. It was just waiting there for me to pull into it. It had our names written all over it, and no one was supposed to have it but us. As Liz would often say, "Our parking angels are taking care of us."

We got out of the car and walked to the front of the car to see why everyone was standing around at the cliff's edge. At that very instant, a whale was ascending above the edge of the cliff ever so gently and majestically and rose higher than we were standing. This spectacular event unfolded directly in front of Liz and me. As the whale slowly dropped back down and out of our sight into the water below, quiet tears streamed down my cheeks. It was as if nature had guided us to this place to show us one more magical event we hadn't expected. Liz and I stood quietly looking forward and staring out at the horizon and frozen in time. I heard Liz softly say, "I can't believe what we just saw."

From above, where we were standing, we could hear the whale below slapping its tail loudly upon the top of the water. It was thunderous, and we counted more slaps than we experienced on our rubber raft tour the day before. Shortly after the slaps stopped, we saw the mother whale and her newborn calf swimming up the west shoreline together.

Kathleen told me she was getting a message from Liz's husband, Bob, "He says he is pleased that you are treating Liz so special and he is glad that you are with her. He is in favor of your trip. He also wants you to know animals are more human than you know."

Kathleen then proceeded to tell me, "You will be taking another trip. Not immediately, but a few years down the line, to India."

I laughed and replied, "India is not a point of destination I have ever had on my travel radar."

Kathleen informed me, "When you go you will be with very enlightened people. They will be similar to the likes of Mahatma Gandhi. You will have to be a student first and then a teacher."

I told her, "I feel like that's all I've been doing is studying since things have been happening to me."

Kathleen replied, "Yes, you have, but you will be taking it up a notch during this period.

After our readings were finished and we were walking out of the building, I asked Liz if she had discussed the Hawaiian island trip with Kathleen and Liz confirmed she had not. As we pulled out of the parking lot to return home for the day, Liz looked to the west and saw a partial rainbow. The weather was warm and sunny, and no rain was in the forecast. Liz continued to watch it as we drove down the road, and I heard her say, "It's a message from Bob."

❦ ❦ ❦ ❦ ❦

On Monday morning while driving to work, and just after my weekend reading with Kathleen Schneider, I recited my long mantra to the celestial beings I acknowledge every day. I asked if they could give me a sign if what was happening to me was real and if I was on the right track. Especially, after Kathleen told me about a future trip to India.

I pulled up to the next four-way stop on Mineral Point Road and Gammon Road in Madison and I looked to my left to see a city bus in the lane next to me move out to make a left-hand turn. On the side of the bus, I saw the words in giant white letters I AM as the bus passed by my car. There was a third word, but it was already out of my sight, and I couldn't tell what it was. I just knew the words I AM were hitting me like a lightning bolt when I saw them. I started to laugh and thanked my celestial team for the prompt response.

The next morning, while driving to work, I again said good morning to all the celestial groups in my daily mantra. I told them I enjoyed the message I'd received the day before. I asked if it would be possible to do this one more time to reconfirm that all of this was indeed happening to me.

I again came to a stop at the same intersection of Mineral Point Road and Gammon Road as I had the morning before. I happened to look down, and the license plate on the car in front of me had the following letters on it: OPEN MND. I laughed and once again thanked everyone for the quick response as I drove on to my workplace a few blocks away.

❋ ❋ ❋ ❋ ❋

Work was busy as usual, and I was closing in on my retirement date two years away. For the last number of years, something was tugging at me deep inside. I often told friends at work, "This isn't where I'm supposed to be." Each year the tug became stronger, yet I didn't know where I was supposed to be going or what I was supposed to be doing. I loved my job and the people I worked with, but the void inside of me was increasing in intensity. I felt like a kitten trying to get out of a big box that had just been put over the top of it.

One evening after work, I met up with my friend Cindy Wheeler to take in a movie. As we left the show house and walked across the street to our parked cars, quiet tears started to run down my face. Cindy noticed and asked what was wrong.

I responded, "Cindy, I can't even tell you anything about the movie we just sat through. My mind was drifting in a totally different direction the entire time." I couldn't explain it very well to her, but she saw how troubled I was; it was a side of me she had never experienced. The hard pull and enormous void had been traveling slowly towards me for the last three years, but now both were about to knock on my front door. *What will they ask of me and what will be my response?*

❧ ❧ ❧ ❧ ❧

After Dad passed away, Mom became my primary focus of concern. Mom's role as wife and companion had been brought to a screeching halt. She wasn't able to communicate her feelings verbally, but her leaning into me for a hug upon my arrival at the nursing home spoke volumes. She hung on tightly and always had tears in her eyes. As we walked together in the hall of the nursing home, I would wrap my arm around her, and she would lean her body against me for comfort.

I continued to visit Mom on weekends as always. We enjoyed going out for lunch and visiting the local Dairy Queen for her favorite dessert. Mom loved her sizeable twisty cone of vanilla and chocolate ice cream swirled together. All was right with the world when I watched her enjoy it.

In the fall, I took Mom for long color rides around the Baraboo Bluff area and visited the Ski-Hi apple orchard for hot coffee and apple treats of her choosing. Winter was more confining, and we had to stay at the nursing home for most of our visits due to weather conditions. During my weekly visits, I would find a quiet corner in the nursing home for us to spend time together. I had to speak loudly for Mom to hear because she refused to wear her hearing aids. I always found a place somewhere outside of her room so we could see outdoors while we shared chocolate chip cookies and looked through magazines for pictures of animals. Mom always responded with soft facial expressions when she found pets in the advertisements.

❦ ❦ ❦ ❦ ❦

Six months before I was to retire, I was sitting with Mom in a quiet corner of the nursing home watching it snow out-side. I heard a soft voice from behind me say, "Good morn-ing. I'm Chaplain Monica Holden. Do you mind if I join you two?"

I turned to see who it was and responded, "Please do."

Mom's face lit up because she was familiar with Monica, and she too was happy to have Monica sit next to her. They exchanged smiles and Mom patted Monica on her arm to show her approval of her joining us.

I had not officially met Monica before this, but she was warm and engaging in her conversation, and she was very familiar with Mom and remembered her times with my dad. During our get-to-know-each-other exchange, I mentioned

I had done a year of hospice volunteer work and how much I enjoyed it. I told her how important my visits with Mom and Dad were as well.

Monica shared with me how she had left her nursing profession to become a chaplain, and how fulfilling it was for her. The moment she told me, my heart danced with joy. Yes, I was paying attention to my heart's call, but never had I thought, before this day, that being a chaplain was a possibility at this time in my life.

When I graduated from eighth grade, I had wanted to be a Dominican nun and enter St. Catherine's Dominican Order in Racine. Dad refused to let me go. He told me he wanted me to live life first before committing to being a nun. I was heartbroken by his response.

Sometimes when we ask for something and it doesn't happen, the Divine has something else in mind for us. It just doesn't always show up at our front door in a box with a pretty bow around it the way we were expecting it. I had no idea if I would be able to get into a chaplain program or not, but I decided to meditate on it and pursue it if it continued to feel right.

✖ ✖ ✖ ✖ ✖

In January 2015, I called Meriter Hospital's Clinical Pastoral Education program in Madison and spoke with the head supervisor, Jeffrey Billerbeck. Jeffrey advised me to complete the application form and submit it along with information about my life's story.

On February 4th, I submitted my application along with 14 typed pages, back-to-back, of my whole life history.

The next five months rolled by quickly and I had not yet heard back from the chaplain program. I continued to hope and pray that my being honest about struggling with my faith would not jeopardize my application for acceptance into the program. I continued to meditate and ask for strength and guidance from my celestial mantra team.

One week before I was to retire in July, I received a phone call at work asking me to come in for an interview for the chaplain program. I hung up the telephone and floated on a cloud for the rest of the day. I would still have to get through the personal interview process, but to be called and considered was enough of an achievement for me for the moment. If it's supposed to happen, it will.

I arrived early for my interview, so the receptionist seated me in an alcove just behind the reception desk area to wait. While waiting, I noticed a tall man in a dark suit with beautiful gray hair walking past the front of the reception desk. My heart fluttered for just an instant when I saw him. I was startled and wondered, *"What just happened?"* Was my heart speaking to me? This is crazy. I don't even know who that person is.

I remembered the first time I felt my son move in my womb on the first day of spring 1972. I described it then as a quick flutter of a butterfly's wings. This too felt the same, only it was in my heart. As I watched the man walk through, he looked down the aisle into the alcove where I was sitting, and waved as if he knew me. Then he continued walking out of my eyesight.

After a short wait, the same tall man I had seen earlier was now coming down the aisle towards me in the alcove. He introduced himself as Chuck Orme-Rogers. He apologized for waving at me earlier. Chuck thought he knew me but had been mistaken. He walked me back to another office to meet with him and Jeffrey Billerbeck for my personal interview.

For some reason, for the first time in my life, I wasn't the least bit nervous or anxious about the interview. There was a genuine sense of calmness around me. As the meeting progressed, I realized I had met Chuck somewhere before. I just wasn't connecting the dots yet, but I never forget a face!

Jeffrey led most of the interview and questioned me about things in my life story. He was holding on to the typed document I had submitted. When I responded to his questions, Jeffrey would say, "Yes, I remember that on page 12." Jeffrey would then immediately turn to the exact page. It let me know he had read my document thoroughly.

The interview had lasted an hour and apparently longer than expected because Jeffrey had to excuse himself due to another commitment. Before leaving, Jeffrey said, "I'm humbled and honored to have read your document. I don't believe I can classify you with any one particular religion. I would have to say you are a mystic. You are living the spirit of the word."

Chuck carried on from there to finish up the interview. During this time alone with Chuck, I realized where I had seen him. Nine years earlier, in my vision of being in a classroom with many people, Chuck was the teacher behind the tall, white, stone table. I was taken aback.

Chuck told me they were still in the process of interviewing and I would be contacted if I was approved. I mentioned to Chuck I didn't think I was going to be called for this interview, and I had gone ahead and made plans for a trip to Florida in November to visit good friends. I asked him hypothetically, "If I am accepted into the program would the vacation dates I planned for jeopardize my being approved in any way?" Chuck immediately pulled out his yearly calendar and looked at the dates and advised me they would not interfere. Chuck then walked me back out to the reception area, and we said goodbye.

I went home and rechecked my journal entry and found the vision and description I had written in my book had been documented nine years before in August 2006. Not all the events in my visions, but a significant number of them, took place precisely nine years after they were shown to me.

❈ ❈ ❈ ❈ ❈

Shortly after my interview, I received word that I had been accepted into the chaplain program. I strongly felt I was now being moved into the spiritual side of my life on the earth. I genuinely believe this was one of the nine gifts Kathleen Schneider had told me about.

I was relieved my Florida trip did not have to be canceled. I was looking forward to visiting with Nancy and Nunzie Basile in Safety Harbor. Nancy wanted me to come and swim with the manatee in the Crystal River, during November. I was thrilled I would be able to experience an encounter with nature's gentle giants.

❈ ❈ ❈ ❈ ❈

My six-month chaplain internship program started. It involved direct ministry, 24-hour weekend on-call duty, supervisory sessions, group seminars, and didactics. During my chaplain training, I was assigned to the Neonatal Intensive Care Unit (NICU) and to help on the 11th floor heart care center, and anywhere else the resident chaplains felt I could be of service and support to them. Chuck Orme-Rogers and Jeffrey Billerbeck taught the interns and residents for the CPE Meriter Spiritual Care Program. My assigned CPE supervisor for the internship was Chuck Orme-Rogers.

I was glad I had retired before taking on this endeavor so I could devote all my energies to the training requirements. My days and nights were filled with classroom work, on-the-job training, and lots of papers to write.

A few months after getting settled in, I attended one of my single hour-long supervisory sessions with Chuck. I could talk about classwork, hospital questions or anything I felt was needed to move me along on my path to becoming a chaplain. As Chuck put it, "I could drive the bus during this hour." We shared our mutual admiration for Carl G. Jung and Chuck shared with me his large red book crafted by the Swiss physician and psychologist between 1915 and about 1930. It was published in 2009 and titled *The Red Book: Liber Novus*.

After getting to know Chuck the first couple of months of my internship and his being fully aware of my spiritual background, I decided to share with him how I knew him during my hour-long session. "Chuck, I just wanted you to know I've met you before this intern program."

Chuck replied surprised, "When did we meet?"

I replied, "In 2006."

Chuck looked puzzled, and I could tell his brain was calculating hard, and he responded, "I wasn't even in Wisconsin at that time. I was still in St. Louis."

I then read to Chuck the entry in my journal about the vision of the classroom and the teacher who met his description.

I never told Chuck about my first day in the alcove and how my heart fluttered when I first had a glimpse of him walking by. I understood later when he became my CPE supervisor for the chaplain program. Another nine-year-old vision and message had been partially fulfilled.

❈ ❈ ❈ ❈ ❈

November arrived, and I flew to St. Petersburg to meet up with Nancy and Nunzie in Saftey Harbor. I left on Friday morning and planned to return on Monday morning so my chaplain training could continue uninterrupted.

Nancy and I had been friends since our high school days. Nancy was a friend you could not see for years, and when we would meet up, it was as if time had never come between us. We always took up just where we left off. Nancy gave me a nickname of "Chappy" when she found out I was becoming a chaplain. She also had a red T-shirt made for me with "Chappy" on the back of it. Nancy has a great sense of humor, and she always makes me laugh.

My whirlwind weekend with Nancy and Nunzie was jam-packed with things to do. Friday night Nancy, Nunzie, and I attended a wine festival in Safety Harbor. We took in all the food vendors and tasted great wines. The Florida weather was sweltering. At 8:00 p.m. the temperature was 90 degrees. We decided to go home to cool down and rest for the next day's excursion to Crystal River to swim with the manatees.

Saturday morning was rainy and foggy. Nancy and I had about an hour ride from Safety Harbor to our destination with the manatees. We arrived at 6:00 a.m. and proceeded to get into our rubber wetsuits, our snorkeling equipment and fins. We took a van to the Crystal River along with three other couples and our personal guide for the excursion.

All nine of us boarded our boat on the Crystal River. We came to our first stop, and everyone got into the water with our pool noodles to observe our first manatee of the morning. Everyone had to keep a proper distance from the manatees while watching them. If a manatee was inquisitive and approached us, we could hold still and enjoy the experience. Nancy was the lucky observer that morning to have an up close and personal experience with the curious manatee.

We again boarded our boat, and our guide took us further down the Crystal River. The guide stopped at an entrance to a tributary being guarded by a man sitting in a kayak. Our guide advised us that retired people volunteered to keep watch at the opening of the tributary that divides the Crystal River from the beautiful secluded Three Sisters Spring. The volunteers watch for the first manatees to enter the tributary to go into the spring. When that happens, no humans can come in until the gentle giants no longer inhabit it. The spring has been known to hold as many as 400 to 500 of these gentle giants at one time. Since there were no manatees in this area, we were all able to swim for an eighth of a mile up the tributary and enter Three Sisters Spring.

This gorgeous crystal-clear playground with its natural fed springs was used by Jacques Cousteau, a former French explorer, filmmaker, and researcher who studied the sea and all forms of life in water. Cages built for his camera crew were still partially visible under the water.

Just as our guide took a head count to make sure all nine of us arrived safely, the sun broke through the rainy, cloudy morning skies. The guide told us we were extremely fortunate to have the entire Three Sisters Spring to ourselves. Usually, other boats would arrive, and the cove would be swarming with swimmers. The weather had apparently deterred other swimmers from going out, and the nine of us enjoyed the exclusive freedom and beauty of Three Sisters Spring.

There were varieties of fish swimming around and turtles gliding past close enough for me to reach out and touch them, as I held myself motionless deep below the water's surface. Trees that had fallen into the bottom of the cone-shaped spring had turned bone white during the years they had been resting on the bottom. As the sun rays pierced the water and reflected off of the white tree trunks deep below, they glistened with blinding bright-white light.

As the sun's rays of light hit the clear water of the naturally fed spring, it looked like long Roman spears shooting through the water from underneath. The sunlight made the spring look dreamlike and the beauty and peacefulness while diving deep down made me think of Mom.

I had shared so many things with Mom on my spiritual journey. The dreamlike world below the surface of the water was just another event I wanted to share with her. I did something I had never done before. I began to mentally talk to Mom and visually describe everything I was seeing to her. The feeling of sharing this with her was overpowering. How I hoped Mom was dreaming and she could mentally hear me and visualize the experience I was painting for her.

I thanked Nancy over and over for getting me to come for this short weekend. The experience of seeing the gentle giants in the Crystal River and experiencing the beauty of Three Sisters Spring and catching up with Nancy and Nunzie was well worth the trip!

❦ ❦ ❦ ❦ ❦

Late Sunday morning, Nancy took me to the most extensive open market I had ever seen to get fresh fruit and vegetables so we could plan a home-cooked meal for Sunday evening, and have some exclusive time to visit with her husband, Nunzie. I insisted on getting a pineapple along with other fresh fruit, even though Nancy told me she doesn't eat pineapple. Nancy and Nunzie used to own the Dixie Supper Club in Port Washington and Nancy had always been known for her excellent cooking. While preparing our evening meal, Nancy showed me some of her preparation secrets for steaks, and my gift to Nancy was to teach her how to prep a fresh pineapple before cutting and consuming it, a little tip I learned in the Hawaiian Islands. Our Sunday evening meal was a feast fit for kings, and Nancy now enjoys pineapple!

Late Sunday afternoon, I received a text message that Mom had taken a fall at the nursing home and was not doing well. I was periodically updated on her medical condition throughout the remainder of the day and into the evening until I could return home Monday morning.

❦ ❦ ❦ ❦ ❦

Upon my return to Rockford International airport on Monday, I drove immediately to Mom's nursing home in Portage. Mom's condition had worsened, and I knew I would not be leaving her side. This situation created another dilemma for me. I knew my staying at her bedside could jeopardize my being able to complete my chaplain intern program. It was a no-brainer for me, and I wasn't leaving Mom's side. Yet, deep down inside, I was crushed that I might have to give up my chaplain internship.

I called Chuck later in the afternoon and filled him in on what had happened to Mom. I told him, "I realize this situation may affect my not being able to complete my internship. Medically, I know Mom is dying, but not being able to put a timetable on just when I wanted you to know I would not be leaving her alone."

Chuck responded in a gentle voice, "You do what you have to do, and we will sit down and talk when you get back."

His kind response gave me a sense of peace and hope. Whatever the outcome would be, I was prepared to accept what was going to happen. I remembered a saying my dad used to tell me. "Once you make a decision, don't look back, just keeping moving forward." Today would be that day.

❧ ❧ ❧ ❧ ❧

I was able to reach out to Chaplain Tom Drury early Monday evening at the nursing home to see if he could get a Catholic priest to come in and give Mom her last rites. By 8 p.m., Chaplain Tom had a Catholic priest come in from the Wisconsin Dells area. When the priest arrived, he was wearing the traditional long black cassock. I was so pleased and honored to see him come through the door of Mom's room in the traditional garb. I felt inside my heart it was a sign of respect for his position, and for Mom as well in her time of need. I so wished Mom could have seen him. Chaplain Tom told me the priest had served time at the Vatican in Rome and he continues to wear the traditional cassock now that he is again assigned back in the United States. The priest, Chaplain Tom, and I witnessed Mom's last rites, and we all prayed together for Mom.

ｘｘｘｘｘ

The next day Mom opened her eyes for a brief moment, and I could see they were clouded over. The medical staff in the room told me it was a sign the end was coming soon. Mom held on until the next night. I had been sitting next to her bed and holding her hand and praying for her when she again opened her eyes. As I looked at her, her eyes were now clear. I stood up and kissed her, then sat down and continued to hold her hand and whispered softly to her. I thanked her for all she had done for me through the years. I thought of every possible thing I could tell her about how unique and valuable she was to the entire family and me. I also thought how I had cherished her presence when I was fighting cancer and her enthusiasm as she walked alongside me when I shared with her my spiritual journey events.

She kept her bright eyes open for 90 minutes. At the very end, I saw tears rolling down her cheeks, and I sensed she had heard my litany of life blessings about her. I stood and kissed her tears. She closed her eyes and passed peacefully into the light of the Divine's waiting arms.

ｘｘｘｘｘ

I was able to continue and complete my intern chaplain program on March 5, 2016, at Meriter Hospital. On my last day, I had an afternoon interview scheduled to see if I could become a night chaplain at the hospital. After my interview, I had to report to a conference room where all of the interns and residents gathered for our last time together at the end of the day. When I walked into the room, one of the residents, John Metcalf, called me over to him. I had worked with John off and on during my internship in the hospital and enjoyed getting to know him. John often told me in group classes that I reminded him of the Apostle John. As I approached him, he smiled and handed me a polished citrine-colored stone with the word "Remember" imprinted on it.

Before leaving the conference room, I also found out I had been accepted into the night chaplain program. Everything I had been shown and hoped for had transpired.

After our meeting, some of the interns and residents went to a local pizza parlor down the street from the hospital to celebrate our accomplishments. The interns invited our supervisor Chuck to join us. When everyone was ready to leave, we all stood outside the restaurant in a row, and Chuck wished us all well and gave each of us a hug goodbye. I was the last person in the row to be wished well and be embraced. This completed the missing part of my vision nine years earlier in the classroom, *when the teacher came up to me, the last person in the first row of the classroom, and embraced me.*

I know my journey isn't finished and this book is just the beginning of another new season in my life and what is to come. Thank you for opening my book and walking with me. Please keep your comfortable sandals as a gift from me and travel the road of love and compassion with each step you take. Namaste!

🦋🦋🦋🦋🦋

"To everything there is a season, and a time to every purpose under the heaven."
—Ecclesiastes 3:1 KJV

CONCLUSION

It has now been three years since I started working as a hospital chaplain, and it has taken three years of slowly putting together the nine chapters of this book. I wanted to write more about my many experiences but decided to stop and honor the number nine shown to me in the sacred geometry vision. I also wanted to be sensitive to the three years of writing time. Things coming in threes always need to be acknowledged.

The events in these nine chapters have all been exceptional gifts presented to me. Right down to the polished citrine stone with *"Remember"* stamped on it from my friend Chaplain John Metcalf. John's unique gift received a place of honor on my computer keyboard during the writing of this book. Many times I looked at it and said out loud the word imprinted on it, and I would be reminded of another event to share with you on the pages of this book.

I fervently hope as you close the book you will feel you have been shown a few unique gifts I embraced along the way: an open-minded way to think, to see how our heart teaches us compassion for others and self-compassion, and a synchronistic event or two, or *three,* that revealed self-healing.

Healing between ourselves and our fellow man, and healing between man and nature, are the key to bringing Heaven and Earth together. We cannot live without either one because we are ALL ONE.

Our journeys will differ, our religious practices will vary, but all of our hearts are filled with the same Divine spark and guidance we are all entitled to. After I stopped questioning and put the "Doubting Thomas" in the box and sealed it, I was able to listen to the lessons I was being taught. In my Cell when I felt I was being stretched to the limit and being readied to be let loose like an extended rubber band, my heart spoke clearly. I was willing to let the wind blow me in the direction I needed to go. I trusted and had faith I would be shown the path that fit my specific journey. It wasn't always easy. Yes, I had doubts, but I kept moving forward. I didn't let anyone who made light of what was happening to me stop me from finding my path.

We each have our role on this earth. I believe many have taken on terrible suffering in today's world so others can be awakened from their deep slumber and see what each of our callings will be to help alleviate the pain and suffering of others through love and compassion. I believe we are "ALL ONE," and therefore their pain is our pain. My sincerest hope is when you hear your heart call, you will be ready to answer.

I don't believe my path and mission are finished, and I look forward to the next "season" of my life and where it will be taking me. My front door will always open to the unique knock that is heard by those whose minds and hearts are accessible. I welcome all those who wish to enter to share the magic of your own journey and its many rewards of listening to your heart speak the truth.

Our souls are here to have a personal adventure and to help us expand into the highest version of ourselves. When you hear your heart speak to you, reach for the stars when you accept your journey's mission because *The Soul is a Living Star!*

Acknowledgments

Thank you to all who are a part of my soul family and for participating in my journey. Without all of you, none of what I have shared would have been possible. I honor each and every one of you with my most profound love and gratitude!

To My Soul Teachers

Julie Tallard Johnson, MSW, LCSW. My heart is open and soaring because of your gifted teaching ability. I can't thank you enough for taking the time out of your busy schedule to write the forward to my book. Who better than you, another Rainbow tribe woman, to help speak my truth.

Beverly Kay, Mystic (deceased). I am indebted to Beverly for her spiritual wisdom and sharing, which I initially resisted until much later in my spiritual journey. Beverly was a pioneer with great enthusiasm who was willing to share all the mystical gifts in her toolbox. She was the first to nudge me and send me a wakeup call when I didn't even realize it was happening. Until we meet again in the light sweet lady! (I honored Beverly by putting the entire recording of my unexpected reading with her in Chapter 3.)

Barbara Krull, Massage Therapist. I'm humbled to have known you for your gentleness and bravery to share your gift of energy healing with me. Your ability to feel others emotional pain and help them to acknowledge it and move forward is a tremendous gift. Sharing your gift propelled me forward to a new way of thinking, seeing, feeling and hearing. You are a gift from the Divine whom all should be so privileged to cross paths with.

Donna Marie Levy, Ordained Ministerial Counselor and Reiki Master. Many thanks for your continued dedication to teaching and guiding so many of those who come in contact with you. Your accuracy and insight into the Akashic records continue to guide me with affirmations throughout my journey.

Joanne Koenig-Macko, International Artist and Spiritual Coach. Blessings to you for sharing your love of art, nature and your celestial connection with the angels to reach people all over the world with your beautiful energy giving artwork.

Arline Rowden, Spiritual and Personal Growth Mentor. Abundant waves of gratitude to you for your continued years of selfless teaching, and sharing of your gifts. For being the first person to use Reiki at Meriter Hospital when most people hardly knew what it was. You are a truly dedicated pioneer. You continue to study the dominant energy centers in the body and the compelling uses and power of the heart. I thank you for being my friend and teacher and for teaching me the exceptional benefits of meditation and staying grounded.

Kathleen Schneider, Psychic/Spiritual Counselor. Many thanks for your years of dedication to your gifts and selfless sharing of messages to those looking for direction. For showing me you are a master of your gifts and for enduring my earlier "Doubting Thomas" tests. You are a force of gentle guidance that opened the door to showing me so much more is available to all of us through the Divine.

Patricia "Trish" Poole, CH, QHHT, RMT, EFT. Thank you for your years of work, study and commitment to helping others to find messages within their past lives and to use them in their current life for direction, understanding, and healing. Your dedication to helping others and sharing your gift is immeasurable.

Kathleen Wildwood, Founder and Director of The Wildwood Institute. Thank you for educating others about the benefits of natural herbs and respect for nature. We need more dedicated stewards like you to teach and watch over the caring of our Mother Earth.

Reverend Chuck Orme-Rogers, Chaplain Supervisor. Your guidance, humor and gentle teaching manner will always have a special place in my heart. I was blessed to have experienced your ability to pull the best out of those you mentored to be hospital chaplains. Please accept my gratitude and thanks to you for your selfless time and dedication to your work in the Meriter Hospital Spiritual Care Program. I'm privileged to have had the opportunity to meet you twice!

Reverend Jeffrey Billerbeck, Chaplain Supervisor (Retired). No words can express my heartfelt gratitude to you for your understanding and openness to have someone like me, who stepped outside the box of conformity, to be a part of the Meriter Hospital Spiritual Care Program. I am forever indebted to you to be able to participate in the love and word of the Divine through service to others. Your mystic friend.

To My Departed Soul Family

William and Dolores Collins. Unconditional love to my birth parents for sharing and living a life of love for each other and family. For being part of the lessons learned during my journey. I'm honored to again thank you both for your committed service to our country during World War II.

Victor and Agnes Lascalle. To my loving maternal grandparents who shared their gifts of unconditional love, laughter, and teaching me the beauty of all nature.

Michael Collins. Dear brother, you have never left my heart's memory. Thank you for your spirit always being with me on my earthly journey. You have been my rock.

To My Living Soul Family

Darcy Lutzow, long-time friend. Thank you for being my surrogate sister, and designated earthly guardian angel with a heart of gold. For gently guiding me back into the world of the living with your healing hugs and heavenly laughter. Thank you for laughing all the way through Ireland with me. We are always there for each other, and the comfort that gives me is priceless!

Kurt Pederson, long-time friend. Your humor and honesty is a beacon of light in the world. Thank you for finding a place in your heart for Darcy, and letting me continue to be a part of both of your worlds. There are not enough words to express my appreciation and love to both of you.

Bob and Judy Broman, long-time friends. For lending me your ears when I needed them and the sharing of good wine, food, and friendship. If the beautiful flowers planted on your deck could talk, for all the hours we sat and talked together, I would have at least three more books to write.

Thank you for sharing your beautiful hummingbirds and all the nature that goes with your charming getaway cabin and the wooded land it rests upon. You know my heart sings in nature!

Elizabeth "Liz" Awe, my favorite cousin Bob's wife and newfound "cousin-in-law." Thank you for all your help and support with this book. Your patience, honesty, encouragement, and candidness in reading over the chapters of the book helped me to grow in spirit and confidence. I can never repay you for your friendship and always being there when I needed a sounding board during difficult times. For sharing your unique spiritual encounters with Bob after his passing, and for including me in your trip to Hawaii to honor your 40-year union of love with Bob. We have so much to thank Bob for. I'm grateful to you for joining the God's country crew in Northern Wisconsin, and for traveling to New Mexico and Arizona to expand our spiritual awareness of the heart-brain connection. Your friendship is unmeasurable and goes as deep as the ocean in my heart.

Bob and Diane Reinen, long-time friends. You are two beautiful people. You will always be my surrogate family. We have shared laughter and tears, and the importance of loving each other in good times and bad. The doors to our homes have always been open, and our sharing of many meals has enriched our years of friendship. Thank you for including me in your adventures and for joining me in mine. Our shared trips to God's country in Northern Wisconsin and our trip to New Mexico and Arizona to learn about the power of the heart-brain connection will always hold a memorable place in my heart. You both have treated me like family, and I consider both of you my surrogate brother and sister. To both of you, I extend many deserved blessings of gratefulness and love.

Carolyn Awe, Educator, and daughter of Bob and Liz Awe. You are a breath of fresh air that added dimension to our spiritual group meetings. The enthusiasm and gifts you bring to the table of our group enrich all of us. Your love of your dogs Colby and Buddy, and your dedication to music and the children you teach makes your soul family beam with pride both here on the earth and on the other side.

Cindy Wheeler, my dear friend and movie aficionado. Thank you for getting me out and away from my computer, even if I was kicking and screaming at times. I miss our sharing time since you have moved to be with family in Indiana. You were blessed with a heart three times the size it should be. You needed a heart that size for all the love you have for your grandchildren.

Nancy and Nunzie Basile, long-time friends. To the many tears of laughter, stories, and adventures we have experienced and shared. To your warm and hospitable manner to guests who grace your doorway and to the unique love you share with each other. I love you both!

MaryAnn and Gary Dennis, long-time friends. Thank you to both of you for sharing your gifts and being the first individuals I ever met with metaphysical abilities.

Mike and Gert Lukens, neighbors/friends. One could not ask for two more wonderful neighbors to call friends. Your connection with Mom, Dad, and me was so unique. You both brought laughter, kindness, and love into all our lives. I continue to cherish the bonds of our friendship, especially when sharing pizza and great conversation.

Sandy Vanko, former boss and co-worker. I am so grateful to you for listening to your "gut" feeling when you interviewed and hired me on the spot for a job. The Universe put the right person on my path at the right time. I'm delighted we have reconnected due to the writing of this book, and I hope to keep in touch moving forward.

Robin Lizowski, former co-worker. Thank you for letting me share your story of loss and for allowing me to help you make a connection through Reiki. This event will always be seared into my heart's memory of just how close we all are.

Monica Holden, Chaplain. Your gentle spoken words, "Good morning" were the beginning of the happiest journey of my life. I am honored to have met you and feel comfortable calling you a dear friend. You are the light that walks the corridors of the nursing home and touches all who come in contact with you. Thank you for sharing Mom's visit. I will cherish it forever.

Tom Drury, Chaplain. Thanks to you for helping me in Mom's time of need, and for sharing time in prayer with her. You are a worthy servant to those you comfort and assist. You and your family are in my prayers always.

John Metcalf, Chaplain. Many thanks to you for your friendship, and reaching out to me in chaplain training to share patients you felt I would be good with. You helped to build my spiritual confidence by believing in me. I will always "REMEMBER."

John LaBelle, owner of the Pink Coyote. The "Three Beautiful Ladies" thank you for making our yearly shopping visits to your delightful store in Eagle River, Wisconsin so memorable. The Pink Coyote is a gift of love to all who enter it.

Larry Cockerel, writer/author of motivational books to help cancer patients on their journey. Sincere gratitude goes out to you for walking into my life when you did. For offering help to bring my book to life in any way that you could, after overhearing two words of conversation in a restaurant, "cancer and book." You too have walked the path and experienced cancer as has your lovely wife Debbie. You live the true meaning of compassion and empathy by sharing your gift of hope, love, and encouragement and making sure one doesn't leave the earth without getting their song of potential out into the world.

Kira Henschel, CEO/Publisher. Thank you for believing in my journey and my written work. My heart can never express the wonder of our first meeting and the words I heard ringing in my ears when you said, "Kathy, I get it, and I understand it." The Universe blessed me with another gift on that momentous day.

Light and love sent daily to my brother, sister, son, daughter-in-law, and grandchildren.

Thank you to all for your belief, support, and willingness to traverse this journey with me. It is a cosmic sharing of hearts and minds that I will carry with me into the light.

Chaplain Kathy Collins, ASC
a.k.a. The Mystic Chaplain

RECOMMENDED READING

Alexander, M.D., Eben. *Proof of Heaven: A Neurosurgeon's Journey into the Afterlife.*

Amritanandamayi, Mata. *Awaken Children!* Volume VI

Berg, Rav. *The Energy of Hebrew Letters.*

Berg, Rav. *The Essential Zohar: The Source of Kabbalistic Wisdom.*

Berg, Yehuda. *The 72 Names of God: Technology for the Soul.*

Boland, M.D., Jean Shinoda. *Close to the Bone: Life-Threatening Illness as a Soul Journey.*

Braden, Gregg. *The Isaiah Effect: Decoding The Lost Science Of Prayer And Prophecy.*

Braden, Gregg. *Resilience From the Heart: The Power to Thrive In Life's Extremes.*

Braden, Gregg. *Secrets of the Lost Mode of Prayer: The Hidden Power of Beauty, Blessings, Wisdom, and Hurt.*

Browne, Sylvia. *Life On The Other Side: A Psychic's Tour of The Afterlife.*

Browne, Sylvia. *Past Lives, Future Healing: A Psychic Reveals the Secrets to Good Health and Great Relationships.*

Byren, Lorna. *Angels In My Hair: The True Story of a Modern-Day Irish Mystic*

Campbell, Joseph. *A Joseph Campbell Companion: Reflections on the Art of Living.*

Cannon, Dolores. *Between Death & Life: Conversations with a Spirit.*

Chopra, Deepak. *Spiritual Solutions: Answers to Life's Greatest Challenges.*

Choquette, Sonia. *The Answer Is Simple…Love Yourself, Live Your Spirit.*

Couch, Stacey L. L. *Gracious Wild: A Shamanic Journey with Hawks.*

Doherty, Jane. *Awakening the Mystic Gift: The Surprising Truth About What It Means to Be Psychic.*

Dossey, M.D., Larry. *One Mind: How Our Individual Mind Is Part Of A Greater Consciousness And Why It Matters.*

Dyer, Dr. Wayne W. *Wishes Fulfilled: Mastering the Art of Manifesting.*

Hanh, Tichk Nhat. *The Diamond That Cuts Through Illusion.*

Hanh, Thick Nhat. *The Heart of Understanding: Commentaries on the Prajnaparamita Heart Sutra.*

Hone, William. *Lost Books of the Bible.*

Ingerman, Sandra, and Hank Wesselman. *Awakening to the Spirit World: The Shamanic Path of Direct Revelation.*

Johnson, Julie Tallard. *Wheel of Initiation: Practices for Releasing Your Inner Light.*

Jung, Carl Gustav. *Memories, Dreams, Reflections.*

Kessler, David. *The Needs of the Dying: A Guide for Bringing Hope, Comfort, and Love to Life's Final Chapter.*

Kessler, David. *Visions, Trips, and Crowded Rooms: Who And What You See Before You Die.*

King, Gofre Ray. *The "I AM" Discourses: By the Ascended Master St. Germain, Volume 3.*

Kübler-Ross, Elizabeth and David Kessler. *Life Lessons: Two Experts on Death and Dying Teach Us About the Mysteries of Life.*

Kübler-Ross, Elizabeth. *On Life After death.*

Laszlo, Ervin. *Science and the Akashic Field: An Integral Theory of Everything.*

Moore, Thomas. *A Religion of One's Own: A guide to creating a Personal Spirituality in a Secular World.*

Moorjani, Anita. *Dying to be Me: My Journey from Cancer to Near Death, to True Healing.*

Nouwen, Henri J. M. *The Wounded Healer: In Our Own Woundedness, We Can Become a Source of Life for Others.*

Osteen, Joel. *The Power of I AM: Two Words That Will Change Your Life Today.*

Osteen, Joel. *Your Best Life Now.*

Palmer, Parker J. *A Hidden Wholeness: The Journey Toward an Undivided Life—Welcoming the Soul and Weaving Community in a Wounded World.*

Piper Don, and Cecil Murphe. *90 Minutes in Heaven: A True Story of Life and Death.*

Rankin, M.D, Lisa. *The Anatomy of a Calling: A Doctor's Journey from the Head to the Heart and a Prescription for Finding Your Life's Purpose.*

Reintjes, Susan. *Third Eye Open — Unmasking Your True Awareness.*

Roman, Sanaya. *Soul Love: Awakening Your Heart Centers.*

Ruiz, Don Miguel. *The Four Agreements: A Toltec Wisdom Book. A Practical Guide to Personal Freedom.*

Schwartz, Robert. *Your Soul's Plan: Discovering the Real Meaning of the Life You Planned Before You Were Born.*

Twyman, James F. *The Moses Code: The Most Powerful Manifestation Tool in the History of the World.*

Virtue, Doreen. *Chakra Clearing: Awakening Your Spiritual Power to Know and Heal.*

Virtue, Doreen. *Healing with the Angels: How the Angels Can Assist You in Every Area of Your Life.*

Virtue, Doreen. *Angel Numbers 101.*

Von Däniken, Erich. *Chariots of the Gods.*

Weiss, Brian L. *Many Lives, Many Masters.*

Young, William P. *The Shack: Where Tragedy Confronts Eternity.*

About the Author

Chaplain Kathy Collins, ASC, was born in Milwaukee and raised along the Wisconsin shoreline of Lake Michigan in Port Washington, Wisconsin.

Kathy is a graduate of Port Washington High School, and during her full-time working career attended Alverno Weekend College in Milwaukee, Wisconsin. Her insatiable love for history was fulfilled by taking as many University of Wisconsin Extension courses she could find through the years. Kathy is an avid reader, loves the game of golf, symphony music, traditional Irish music, and enjoys traveling in and out of the country meeting new people.

Her life experiences of working in the business world, being a volunteer hospice caregiver, and surviving her own personal fight with cancer, gave Kathy the tools to fulfill her spiritual journey of transformation to becoming a hospital chaplain. She continues to share the beauty of bringing Heaven and Earth together without fear and showing us how much we are all one.

Kathy continues her mystical journey through the heart by continuing to write, speak and fulfill her chaplain duties. She now resides in Sun Prairie, Wisconsin.

Contact Info:
https://kathycollinswriter.com
kathycollinswriter@gmail.com